AF487548

TRUST IN GOD

INSPIRATIONAL QUOTES FROM THE BIBLE

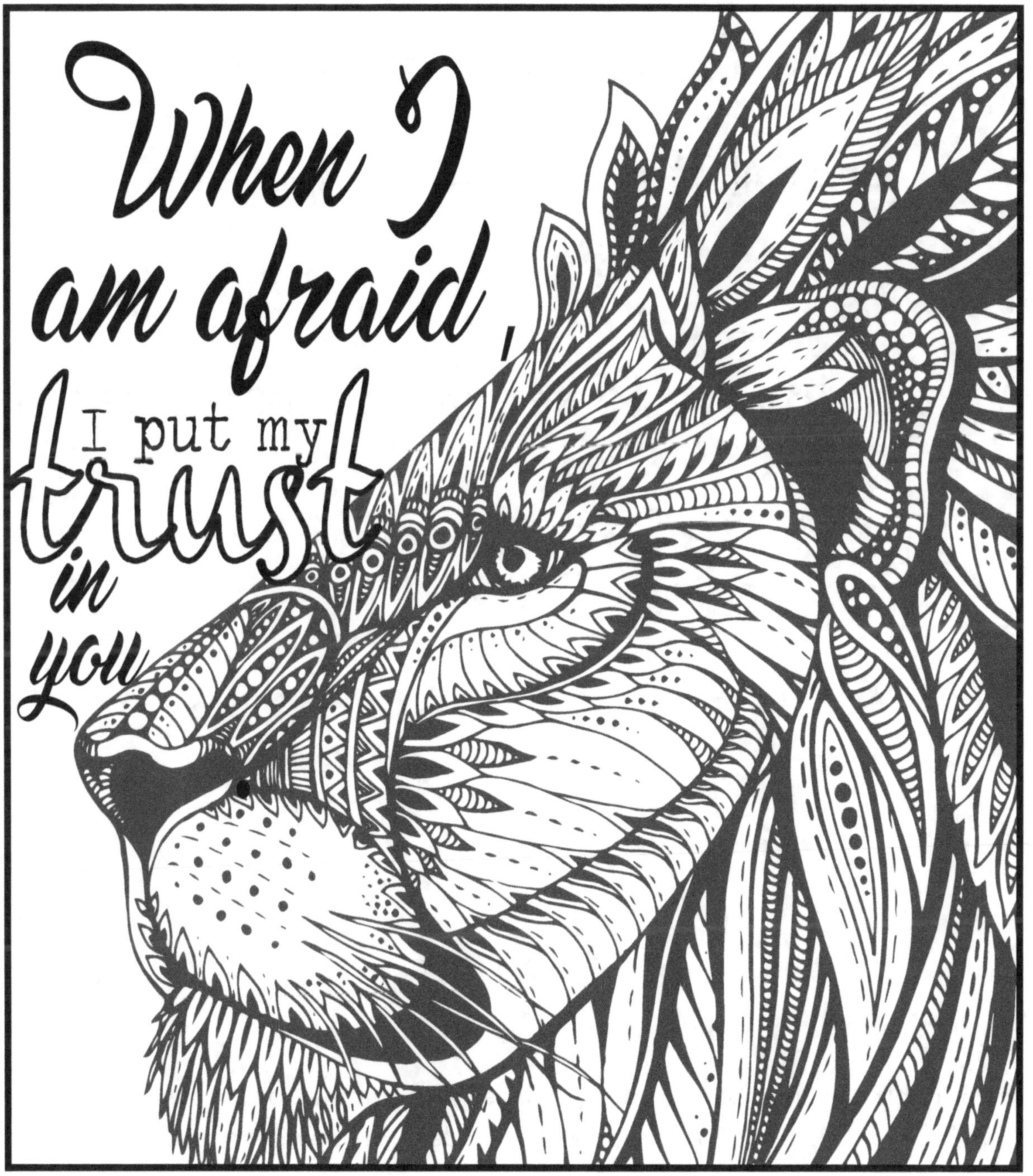

Hue Coloring

Let us feature your completed coloring page

on our Facebook page:

https://www.facebook.com/huecoloring

Send your work of art via private message to

https://www.facebook.com/huecoloring

or email it to huecoloringbooks@gmail.com.

We would love to see your masterpieces!

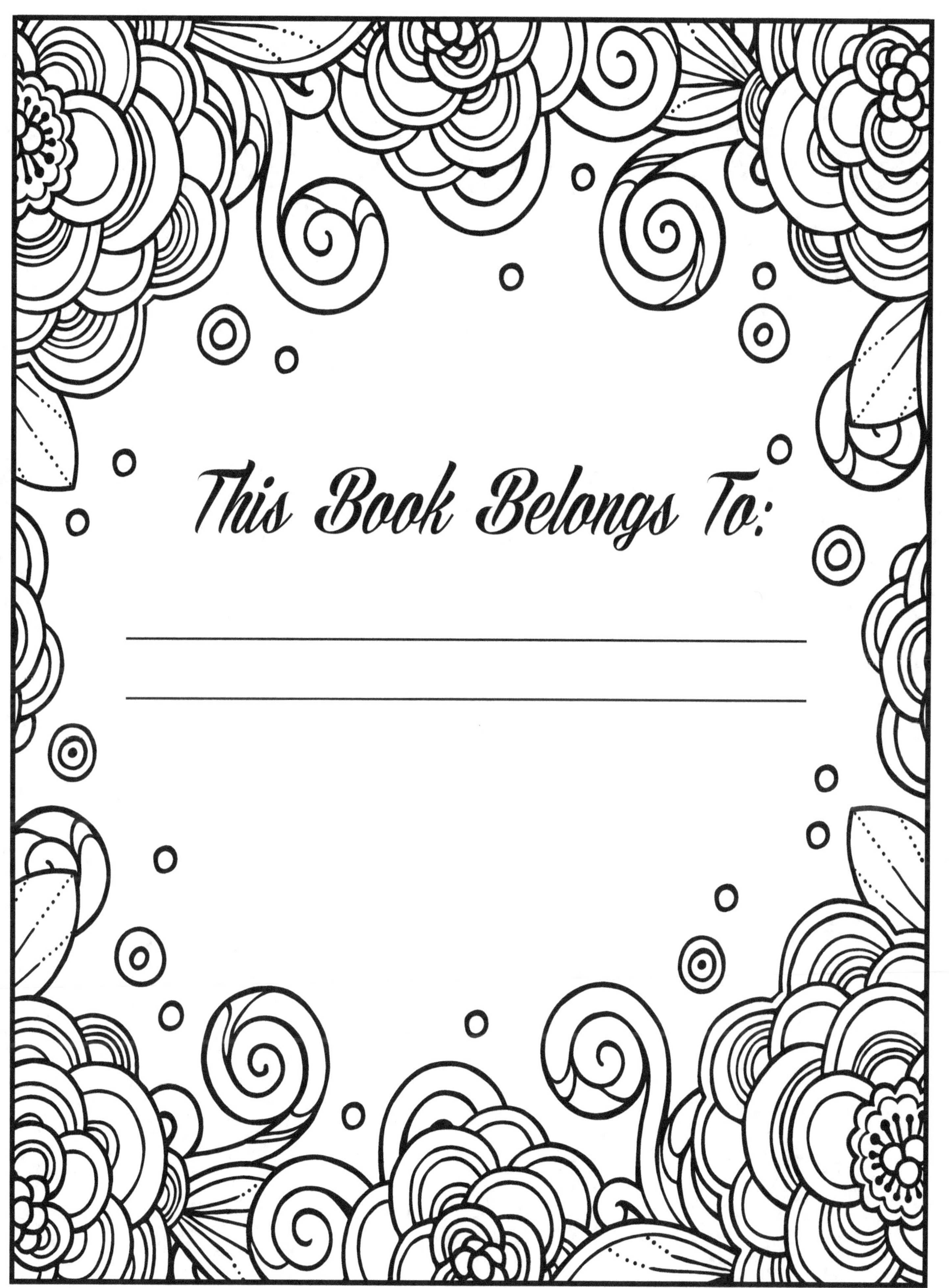

This Book Belongs To:

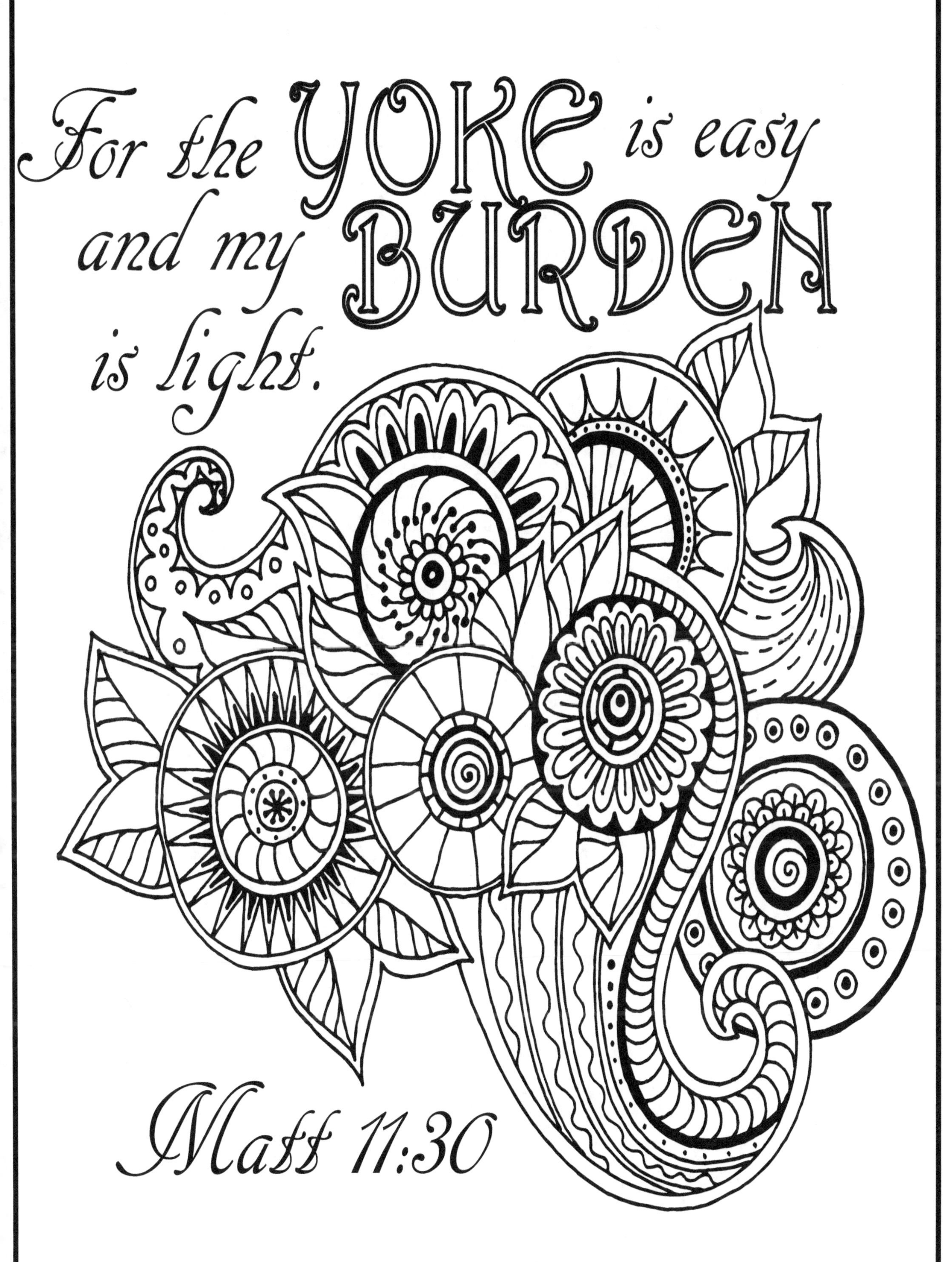

For the YOKE is easy
and my BURDEN
is light.
Matt 11:30

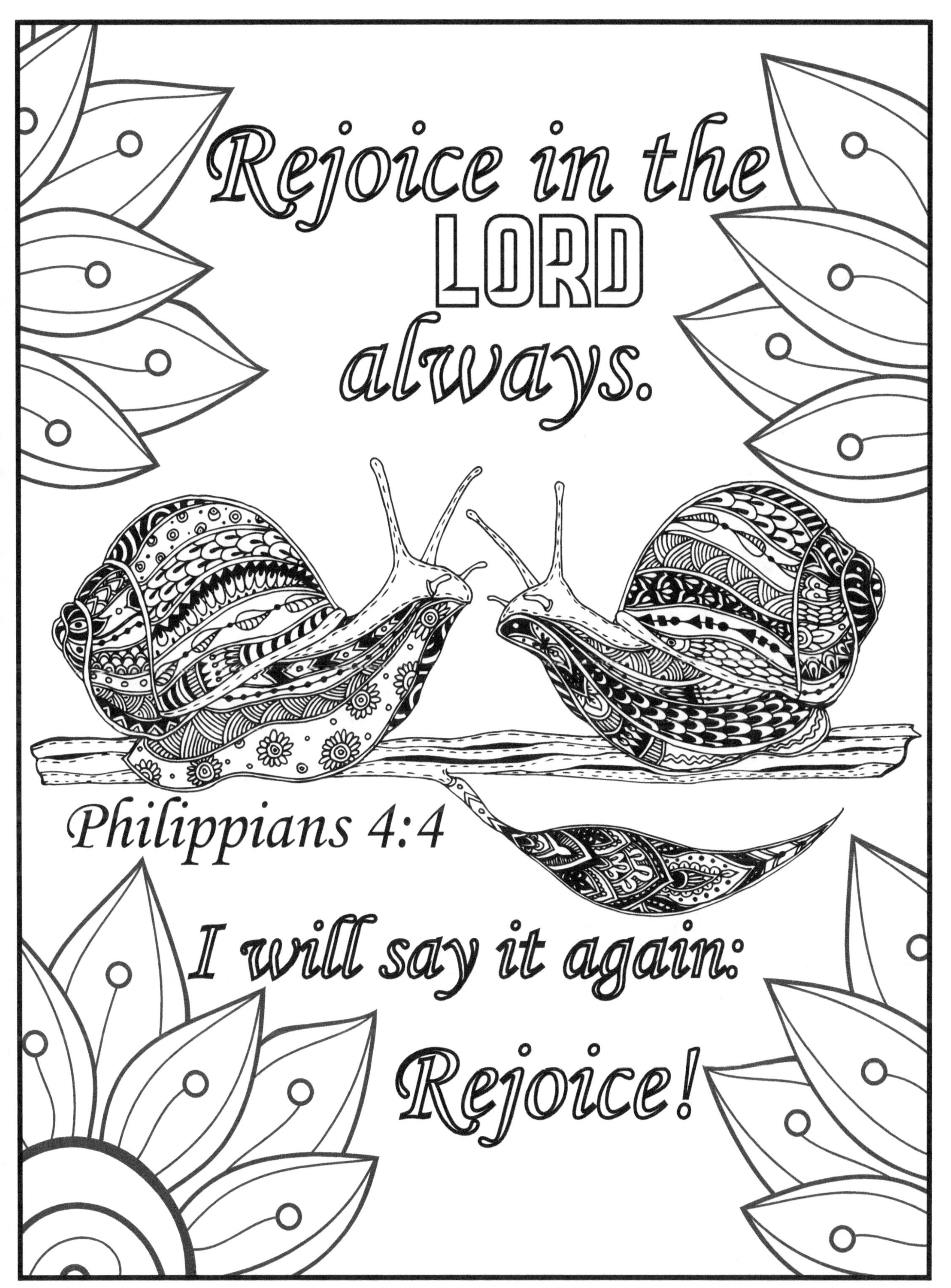

Rejoice in the LORD always.
Philippians 4:4
I will say it again: Rejoice!

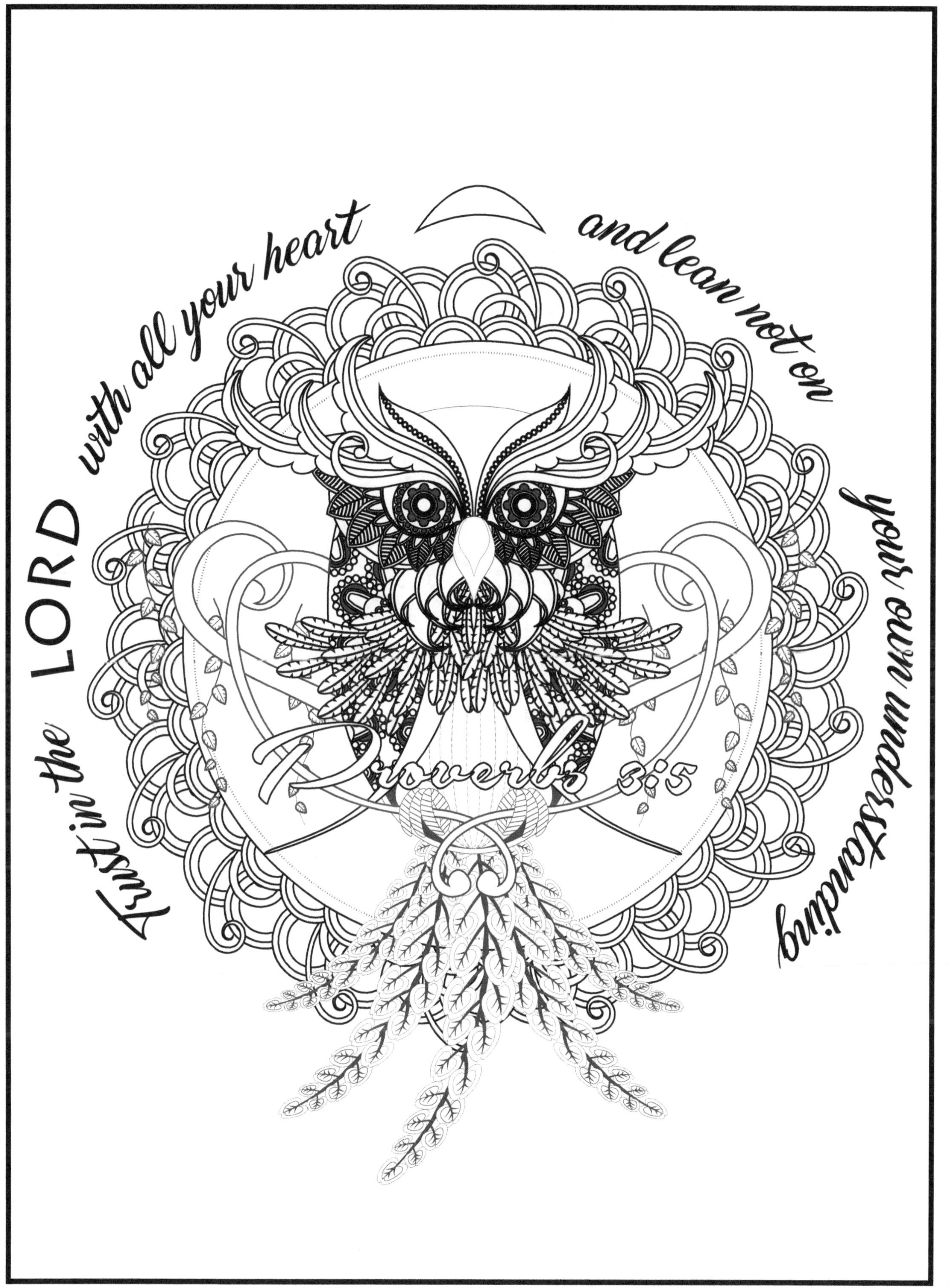

Trust in the LORD with all your heart
and lean not on your own understanding
Proverbs 3:5

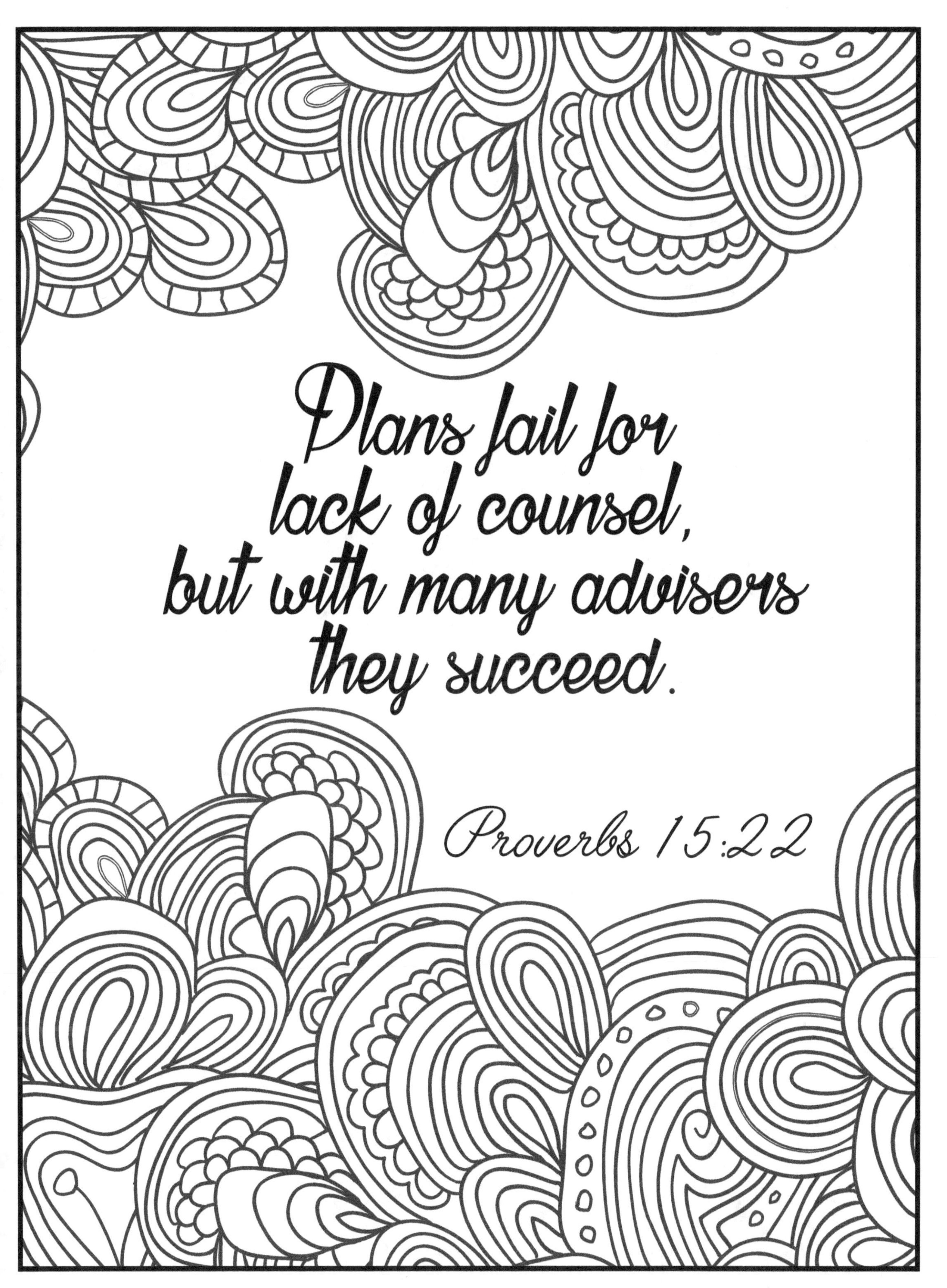

Plans fail for
lack of counsel,
but with many advisers
they succeed.

Proverbs 15:22

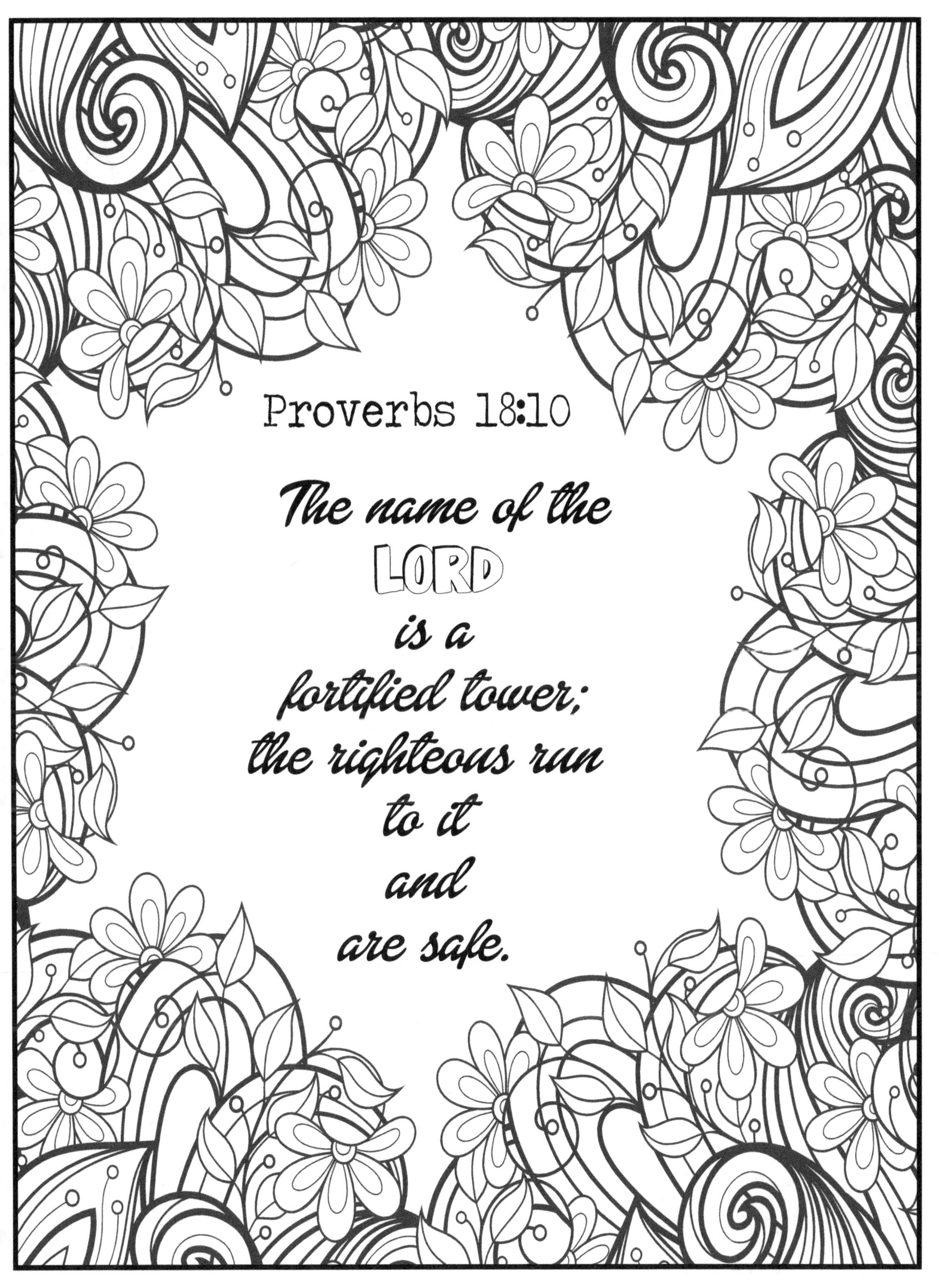

Proverbs 18:10
The name of the
LORD
is a
fortified tower;
the righteous run
to it
and
are safe.

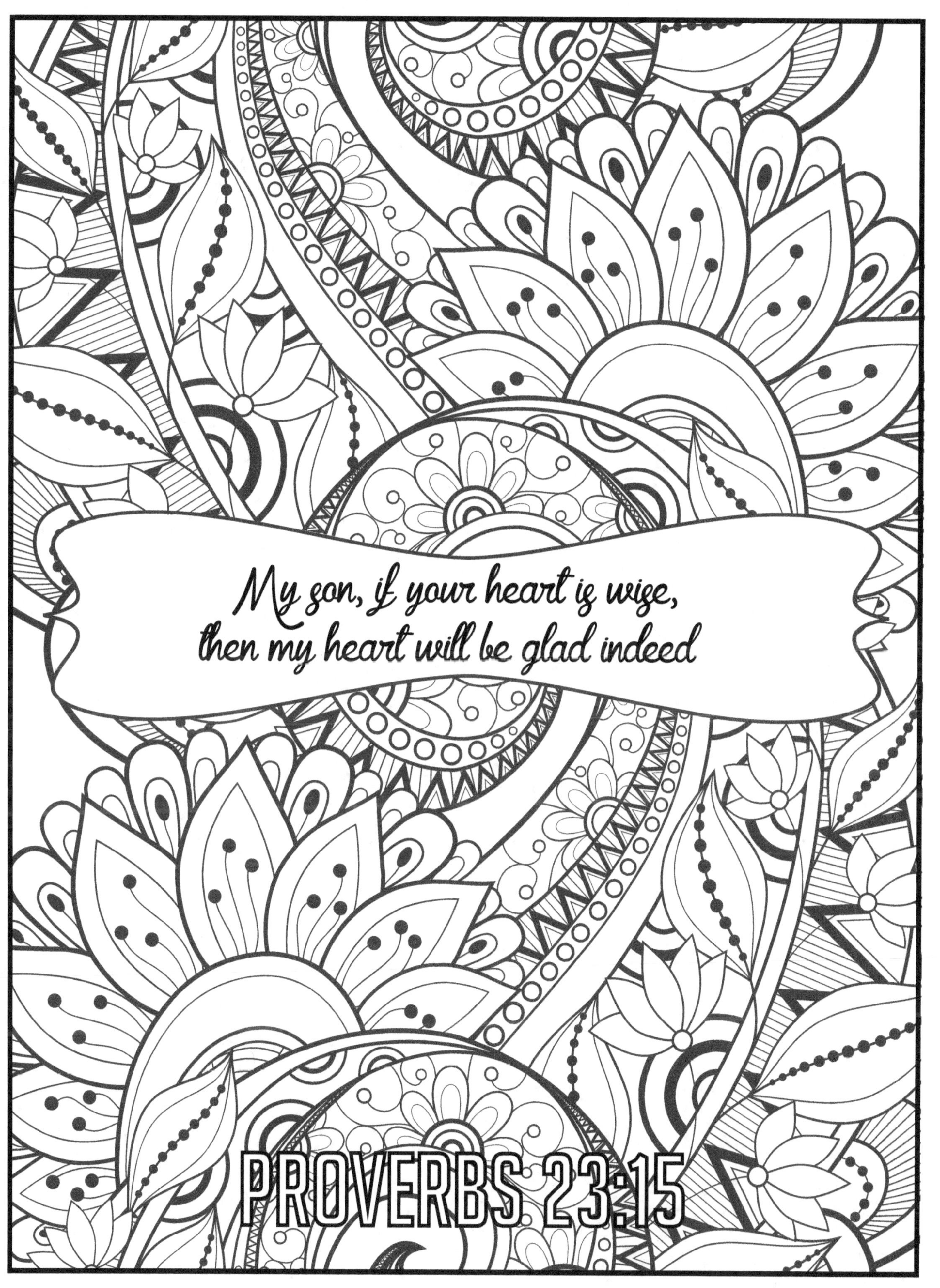

My son, if your heart is wise,
then my heart will be glad indeed
PROVERBS 23:15

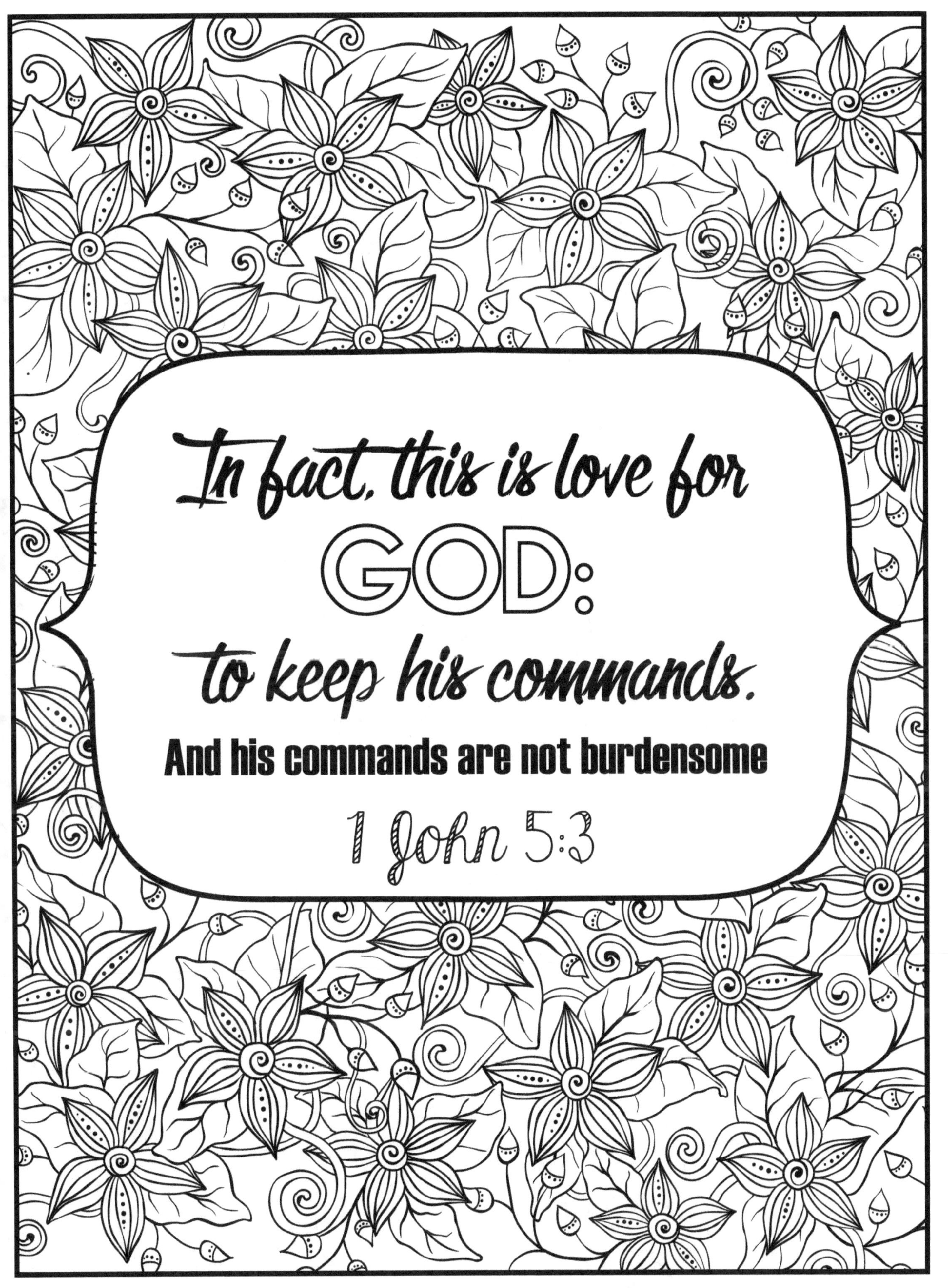

In fact, this is love for GOD: to keep his commands.
And his commands are not burdensome
1 John 5:3

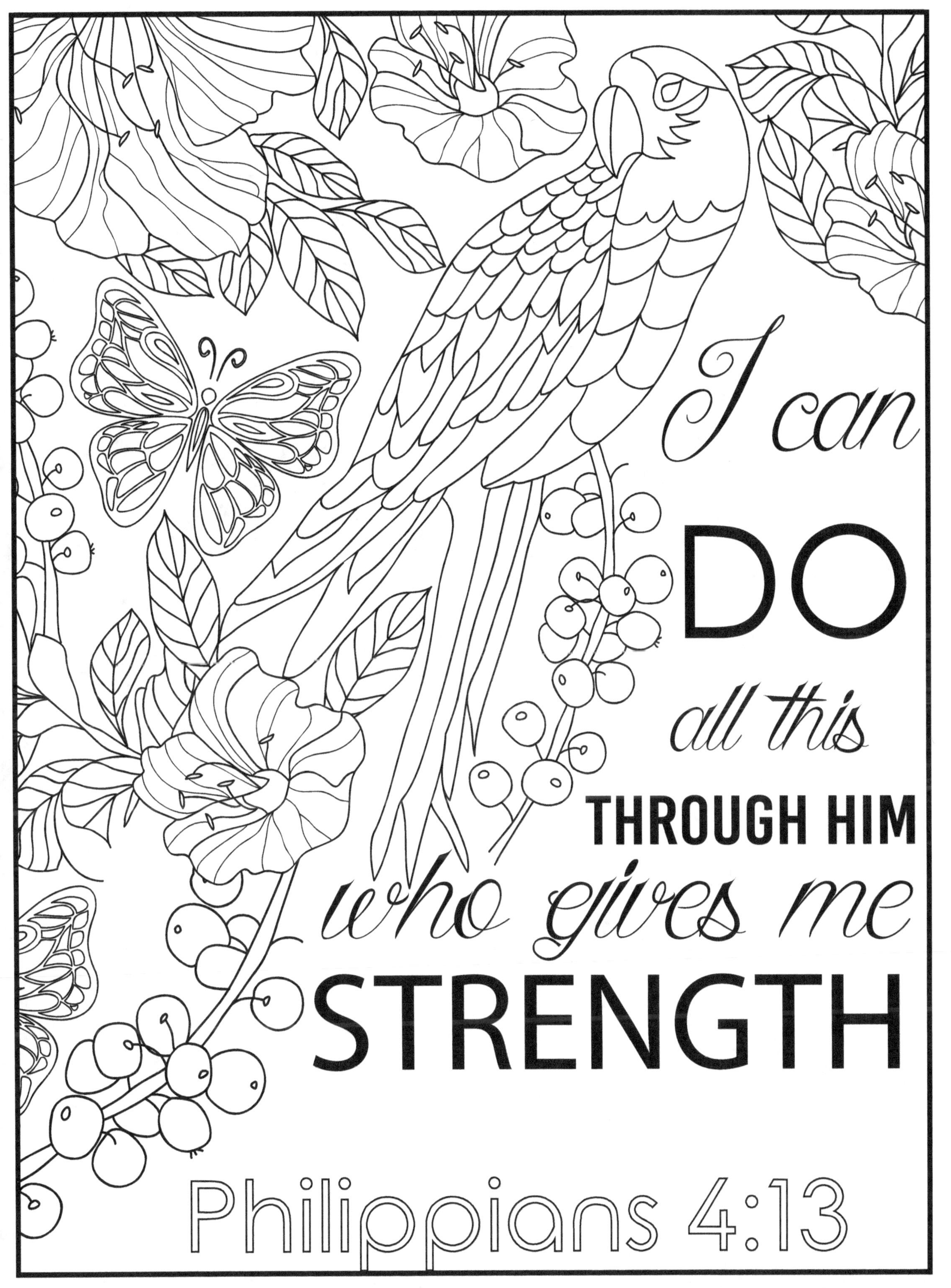

I can
DO
all this
THROUGH HIM
who gives me
STRENGTH
Philippians 4:13

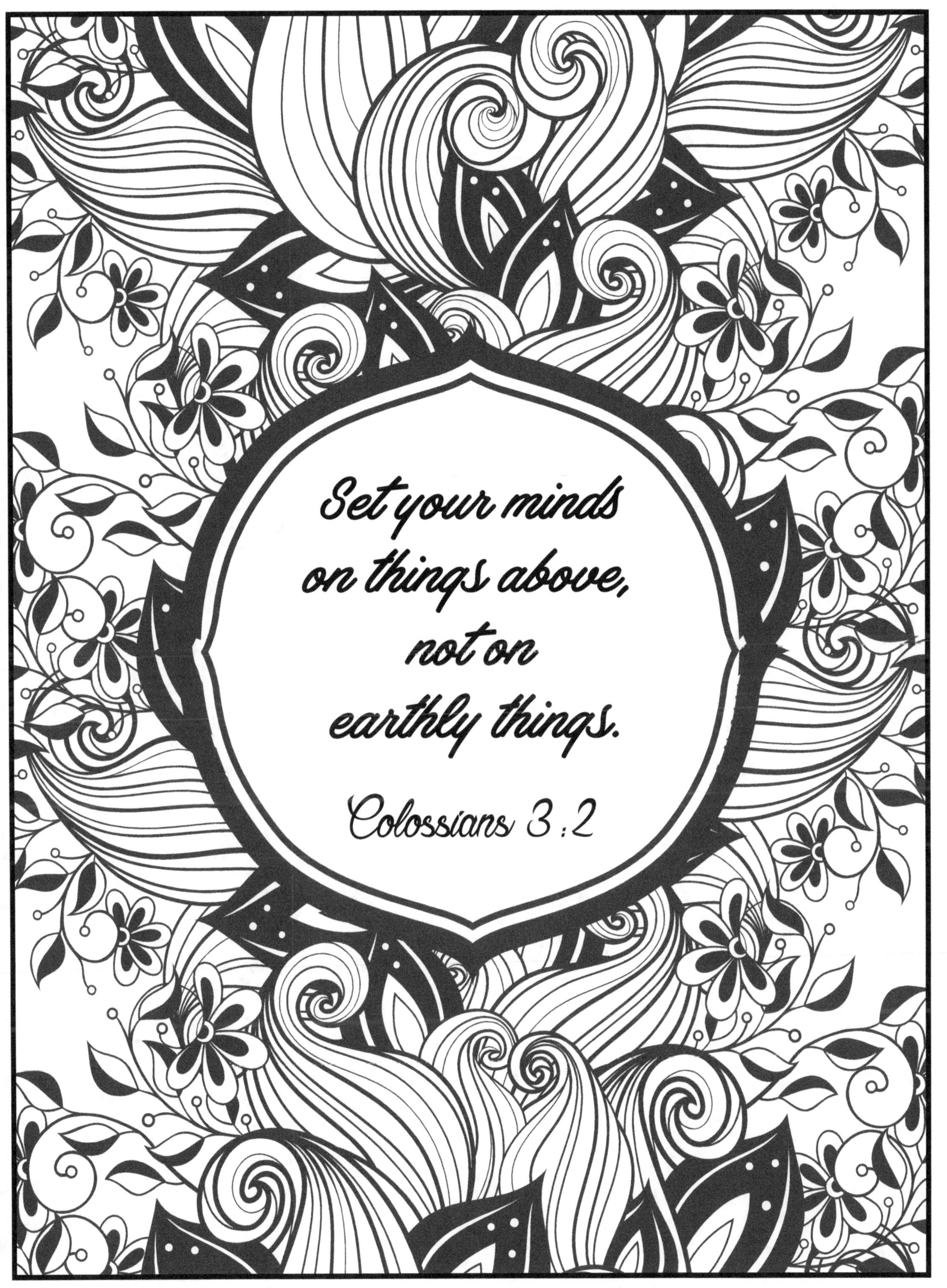
Set your minds
on things above,
not on
earthly things.

Colossians 3 : 2

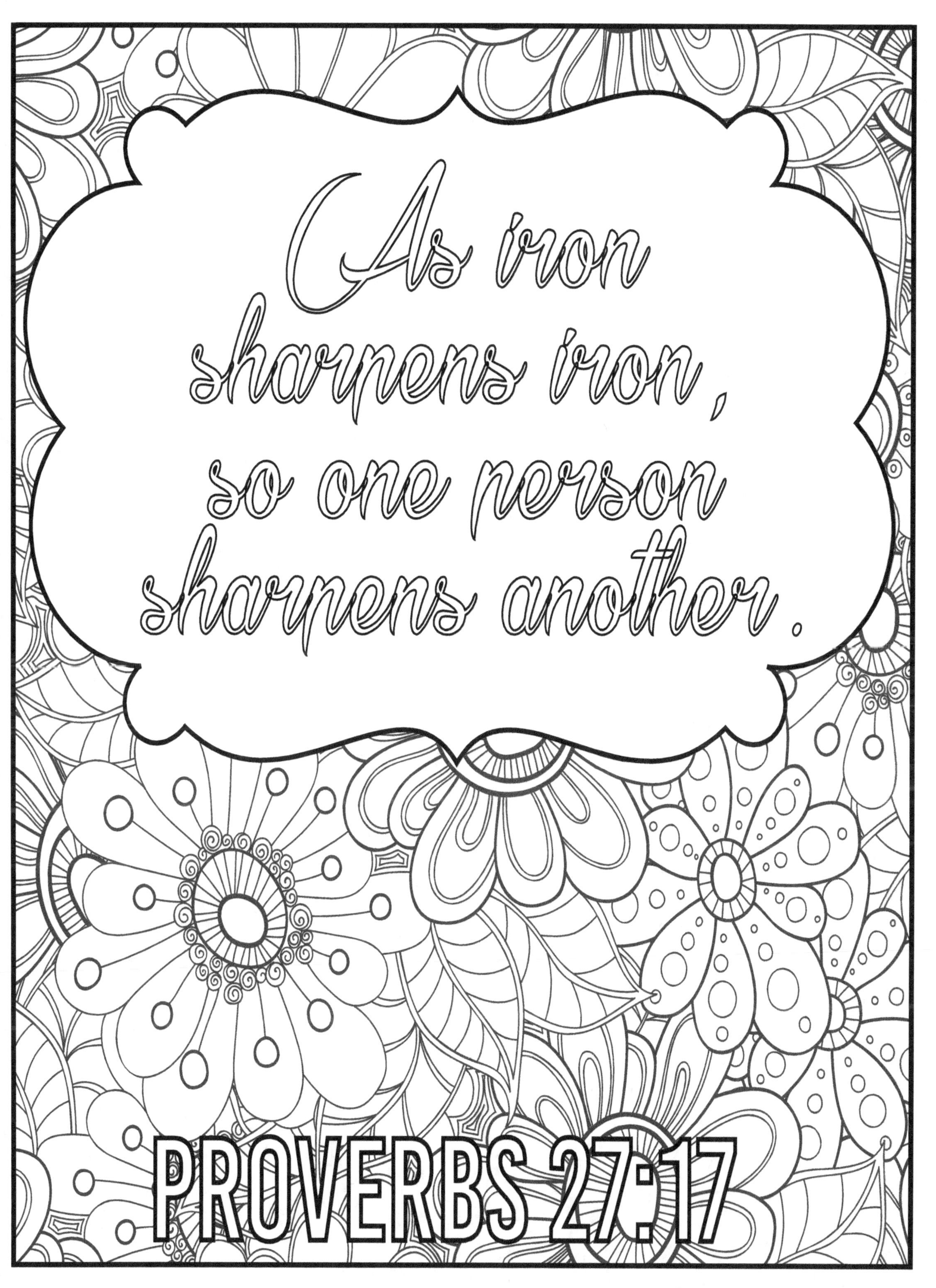

As iron sharpens iron, so one person sharpens another.
PROVERBS 27:17

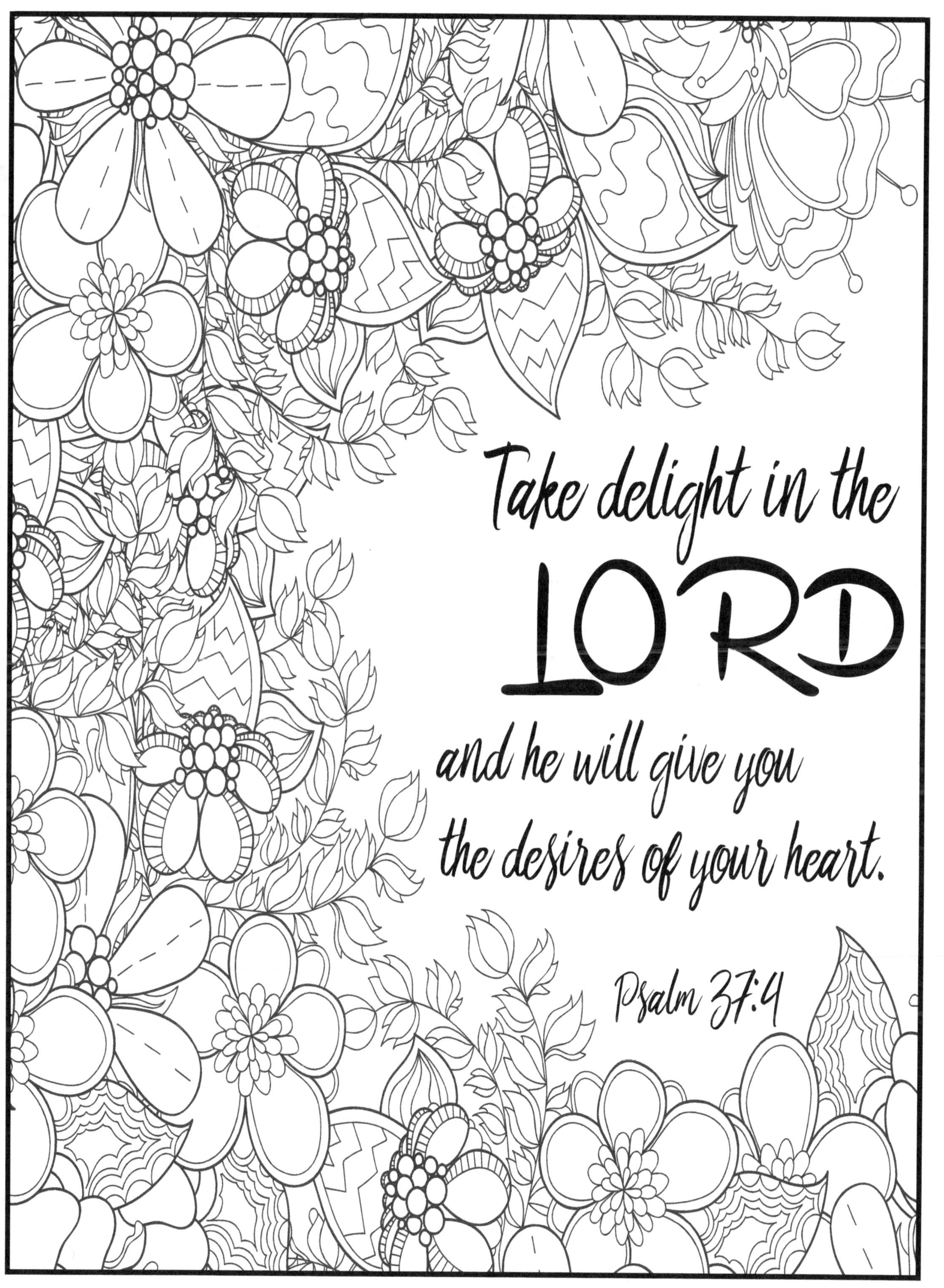

Take delight in the
LORD
and he will give you
the desires of your heart.
Psalm 37:4

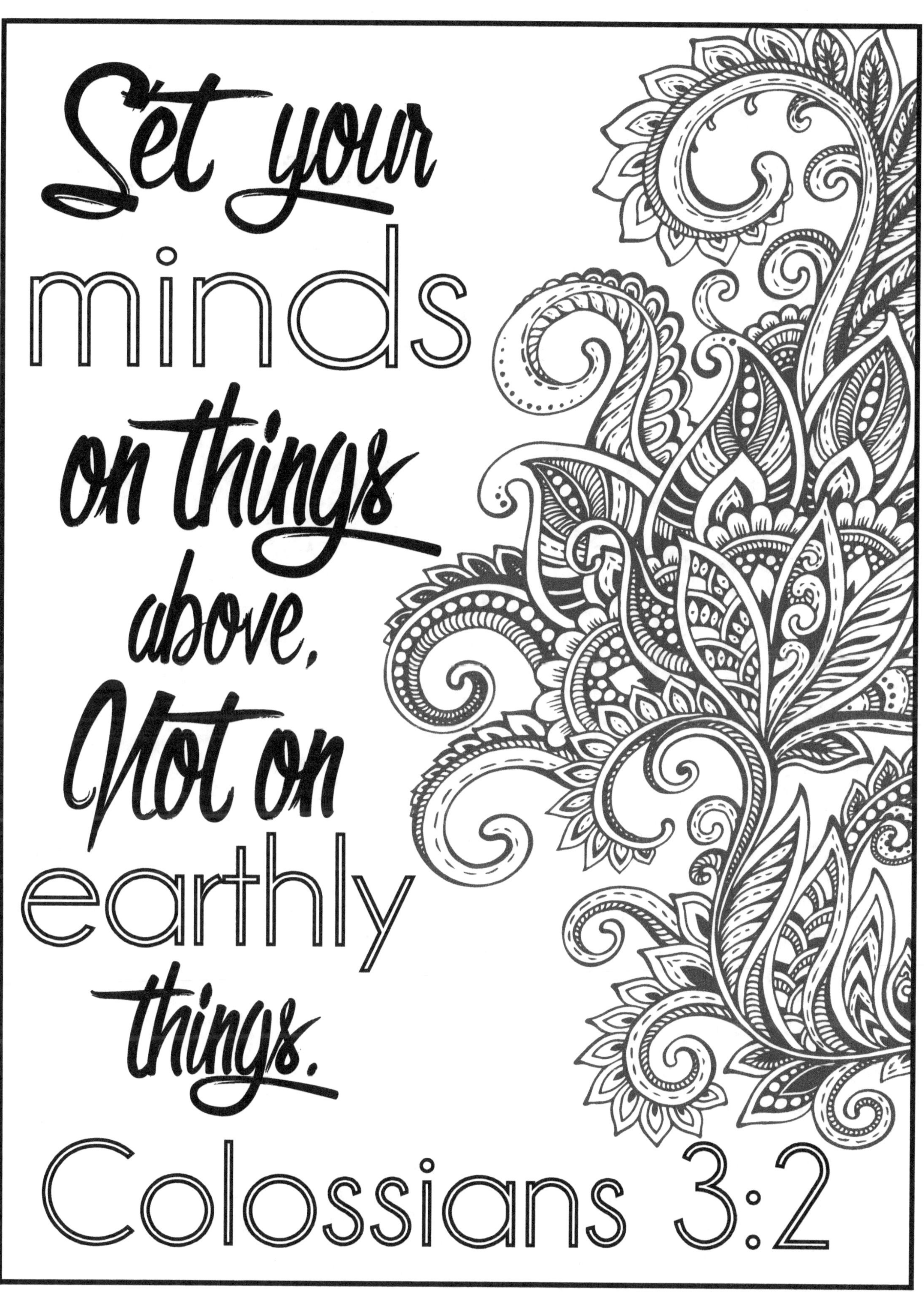

Set your minds on things above, Not on earthly things.
Colossians 3:2

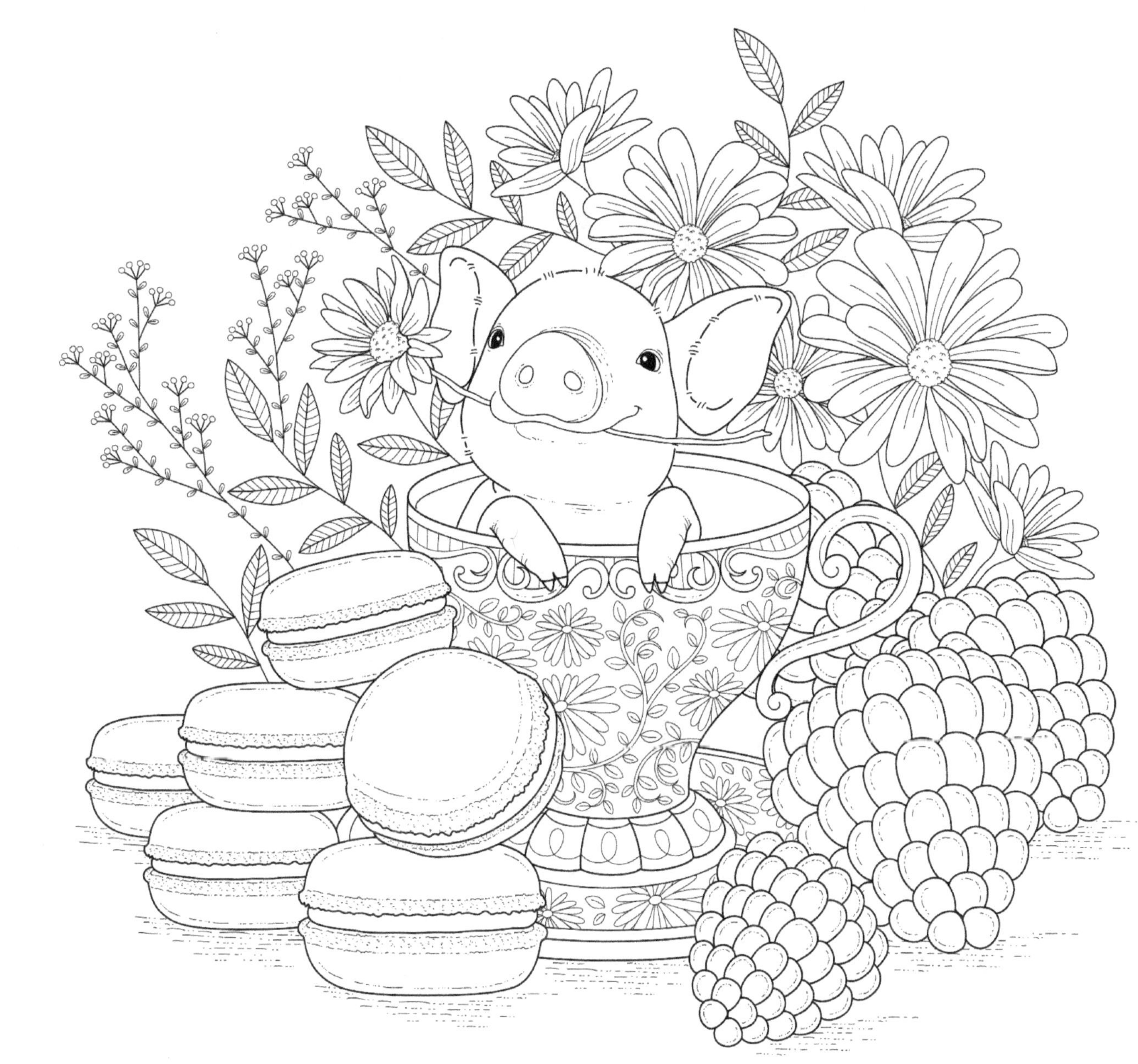

Your word is a lamp for my feet,
a light on my path.

Psalm 119:105

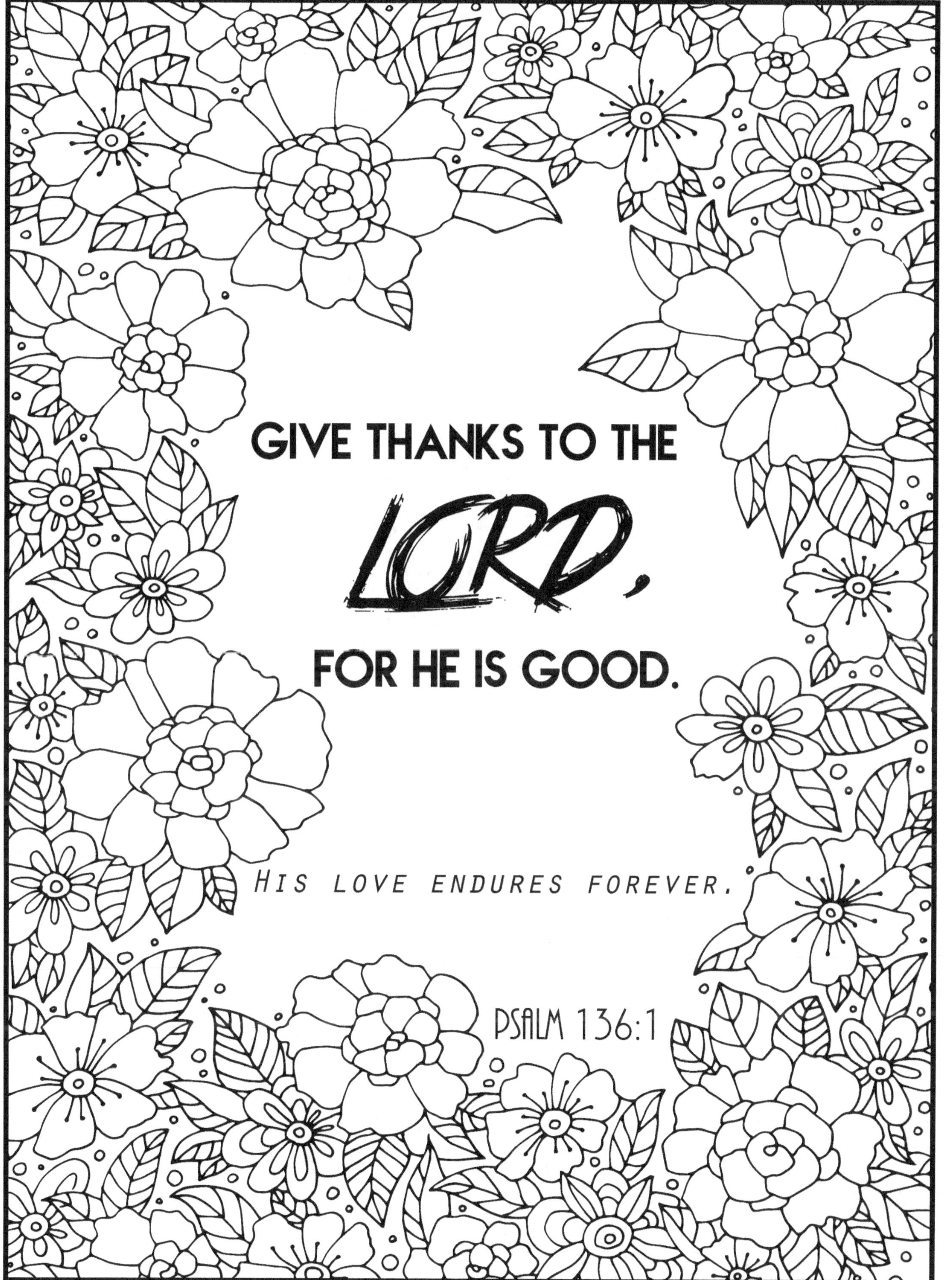

GIVE THANKS TO THE
LORD,
FOR HE IS GOOD.
HIS LOVE ENDURES FOREVER.
PSALM 136:1

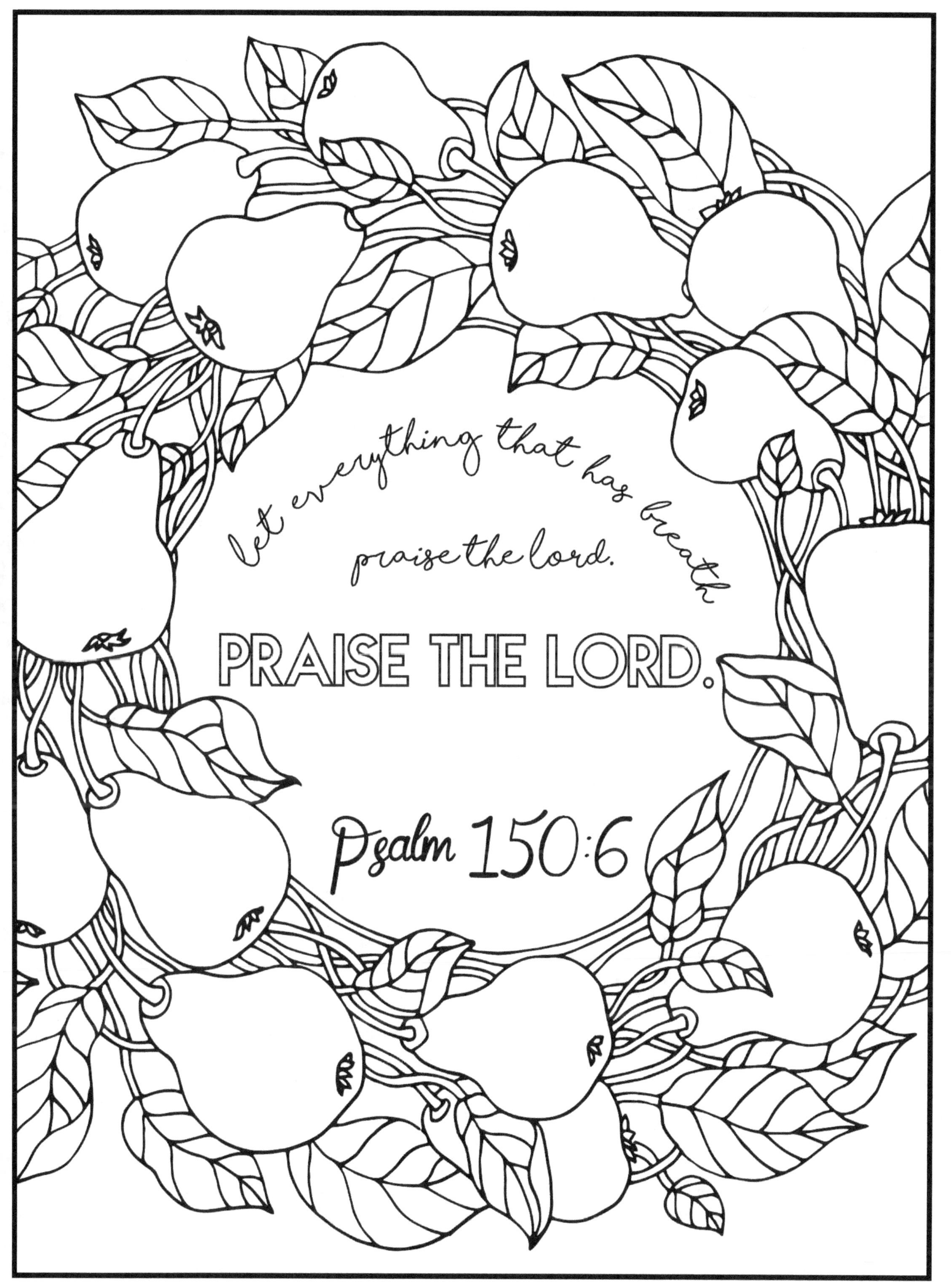

Let everything that has breath praise the lord.
PRAISE THE LORD.
Psalm 150:6

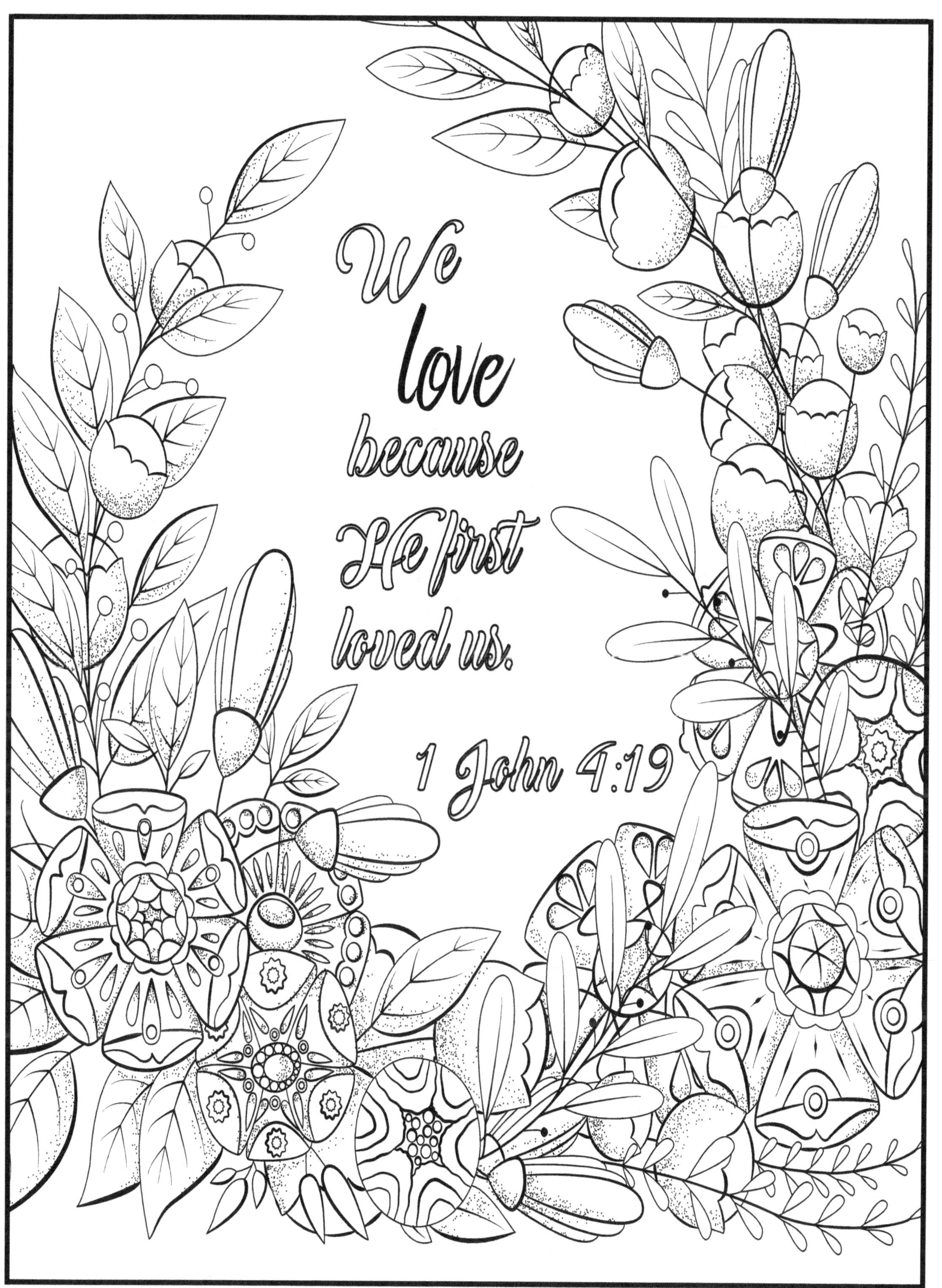

We
love
because
He first
loved us.

1 John 4:19

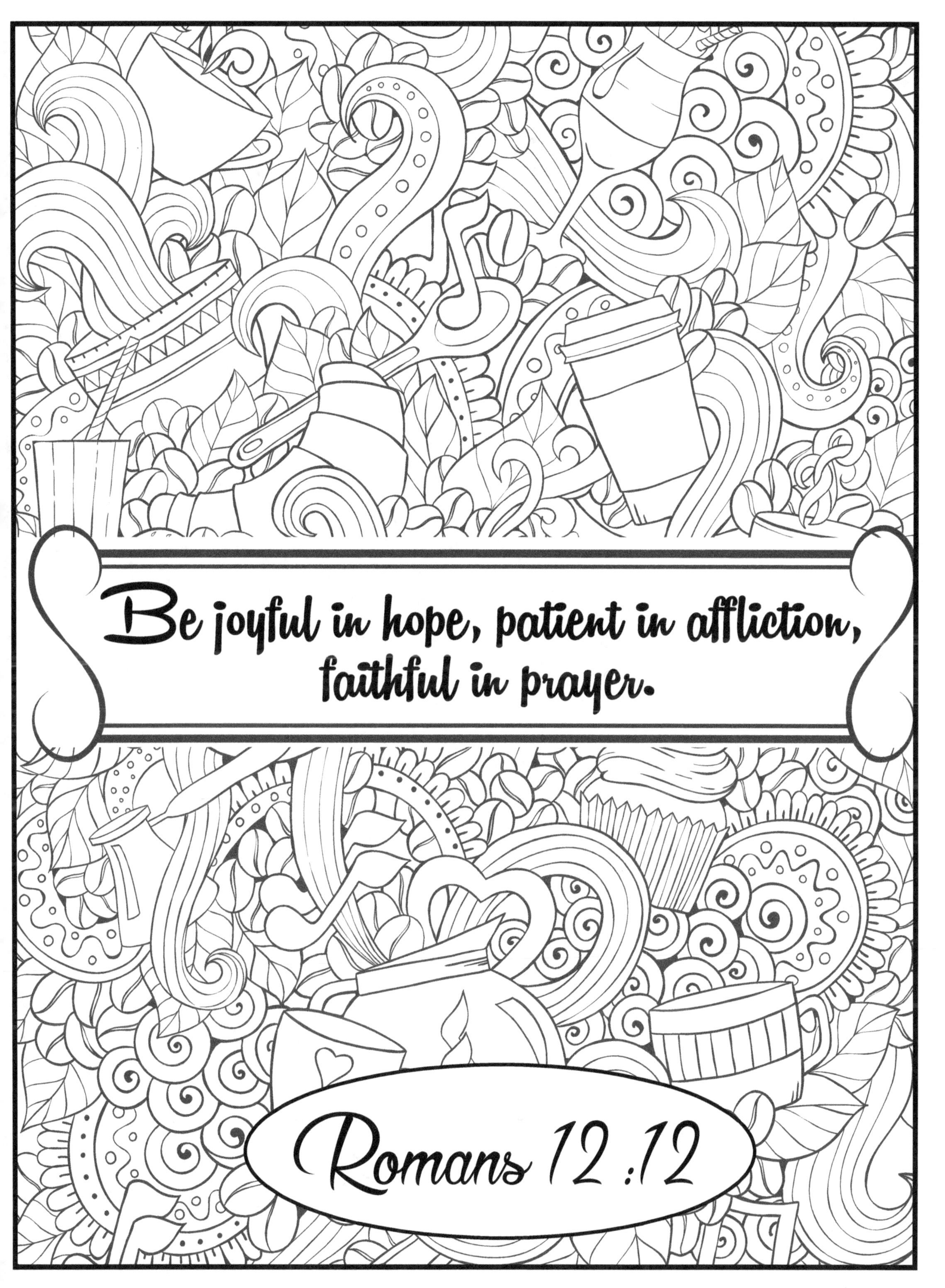Be joyful in hope, patient in affliction, faithful in prayer.
Romans 12 :12

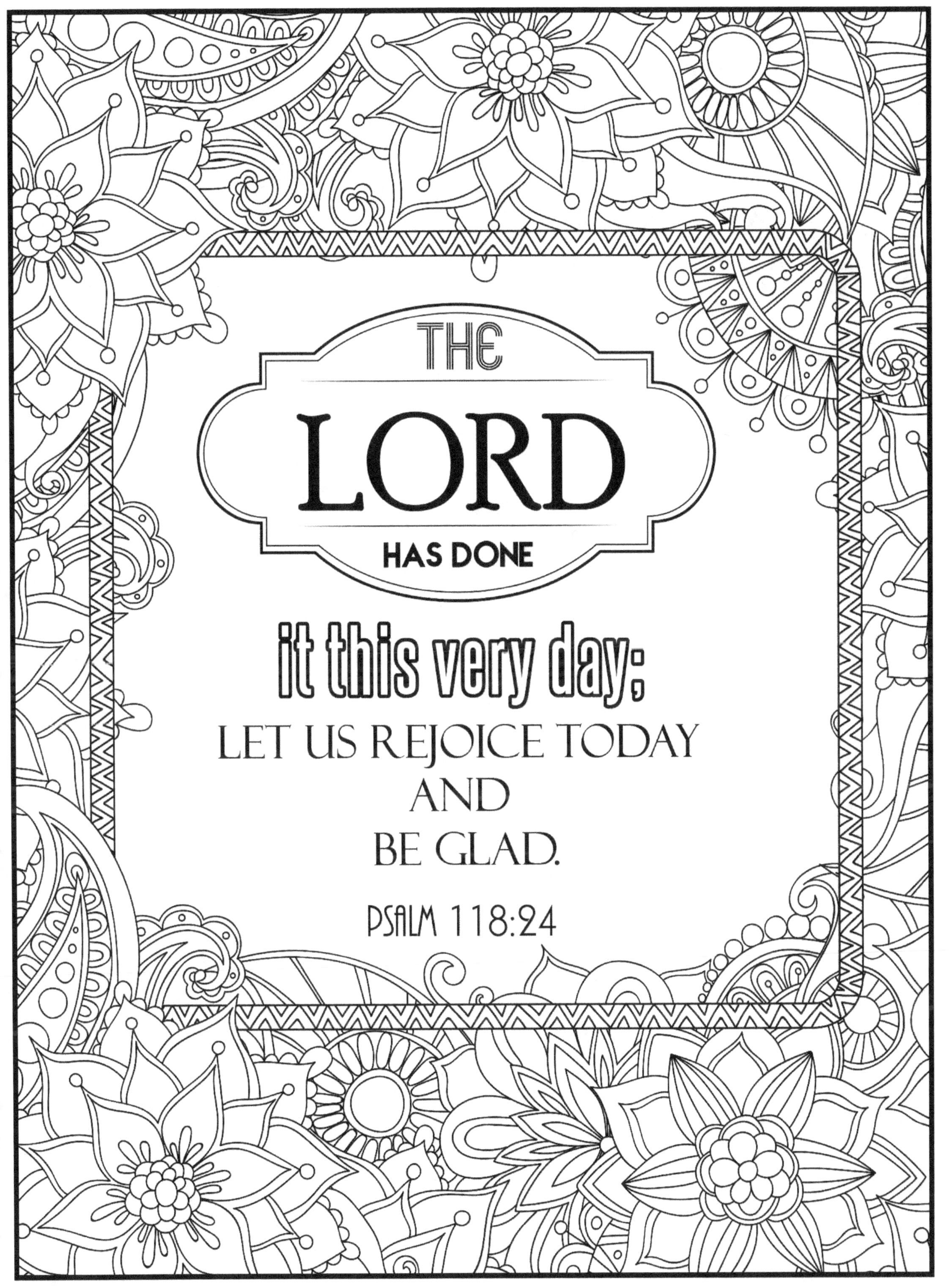
THE
LORD
HAS DONE
it this very day;
LET US REJOICE TODAY
AND
BE GLAD.
PSALM 118:24

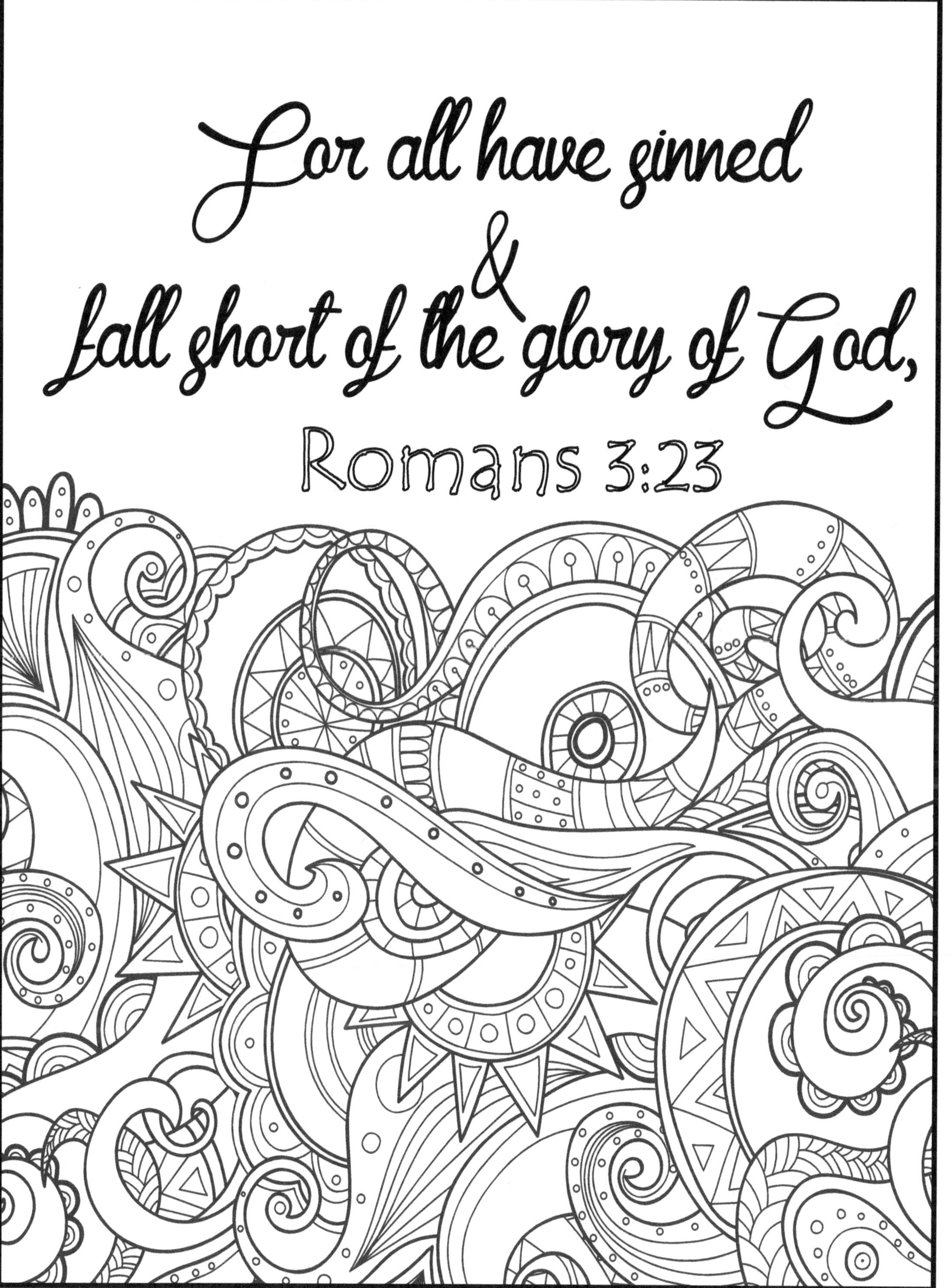
For all have sinned
&
fall short of the glory of God,
Romans 3:23

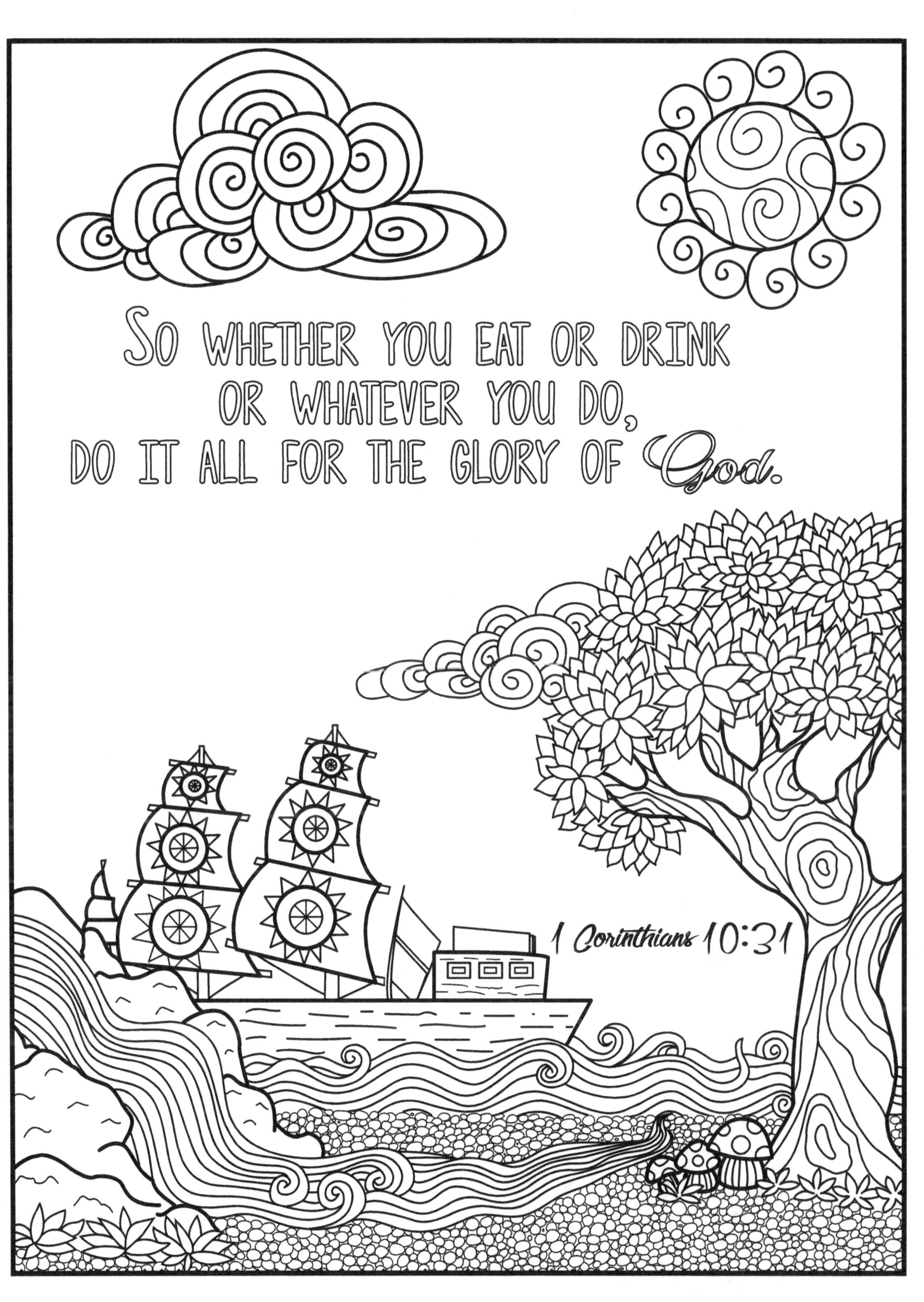

So whether you eat or drink
or whatever you do,
do it all for the glory of God.
1 Corinthians 10:31

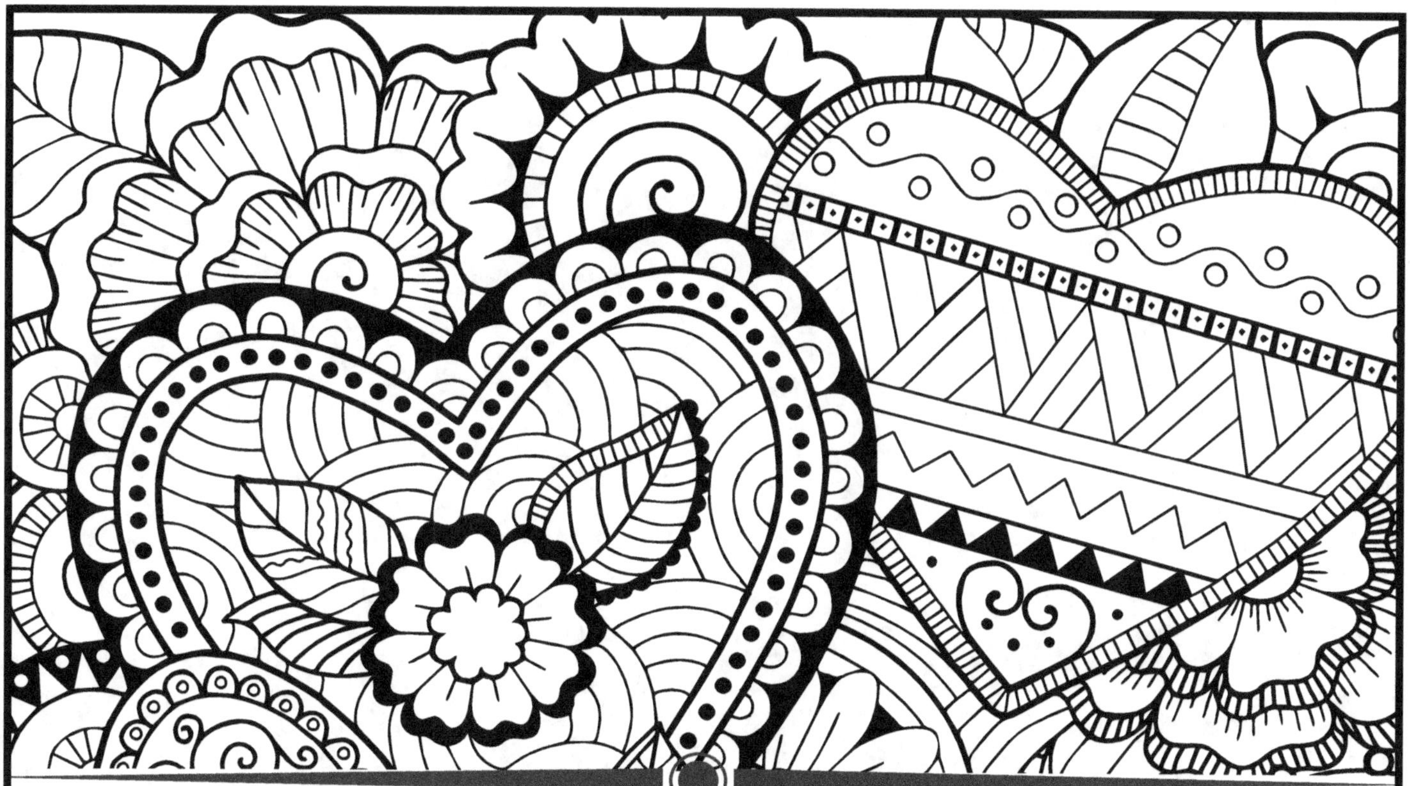

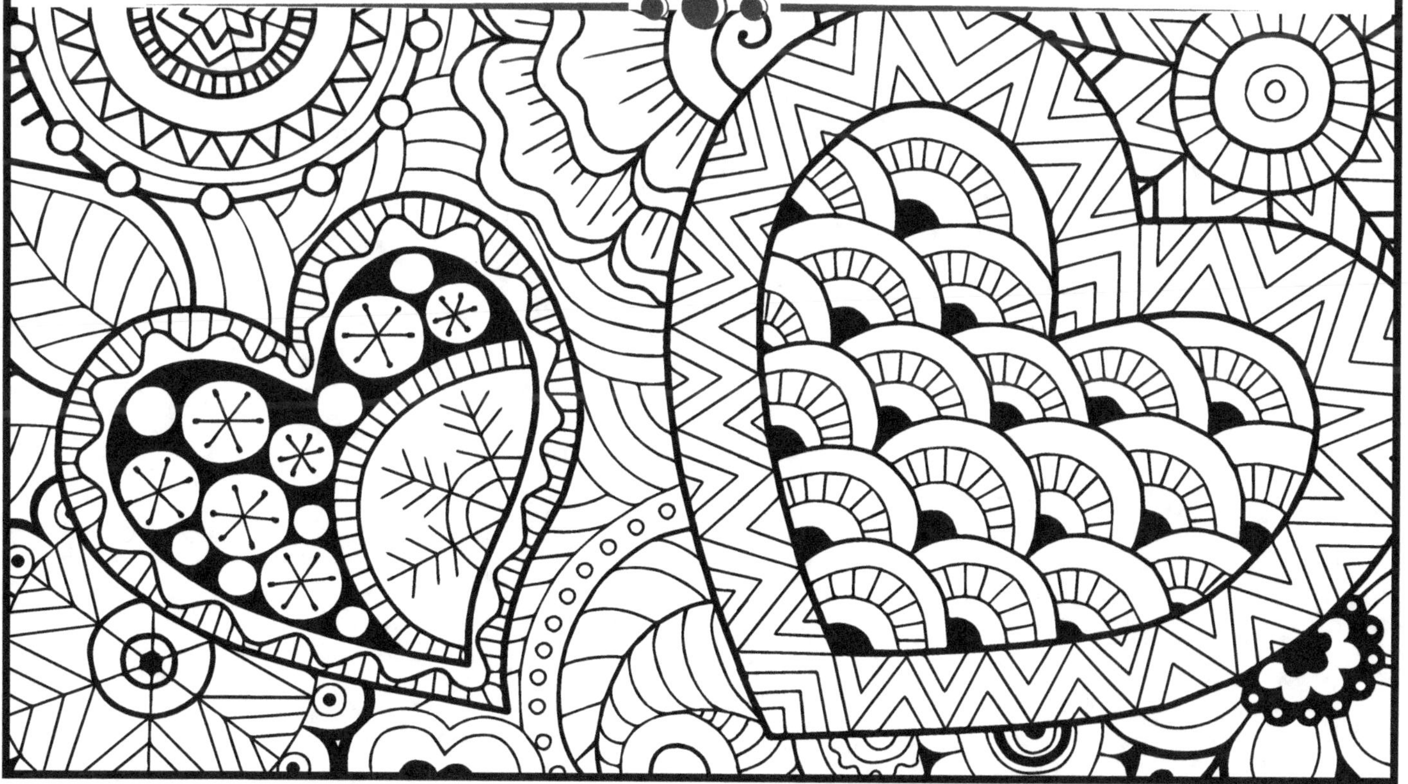

Hebrews 11:1
Now faith is confidence in what we hope for
&
assurance about what we do not see.

Hatred stirs up conflict,
but *love* covers over
all wrongs.

Proverbs 10:12

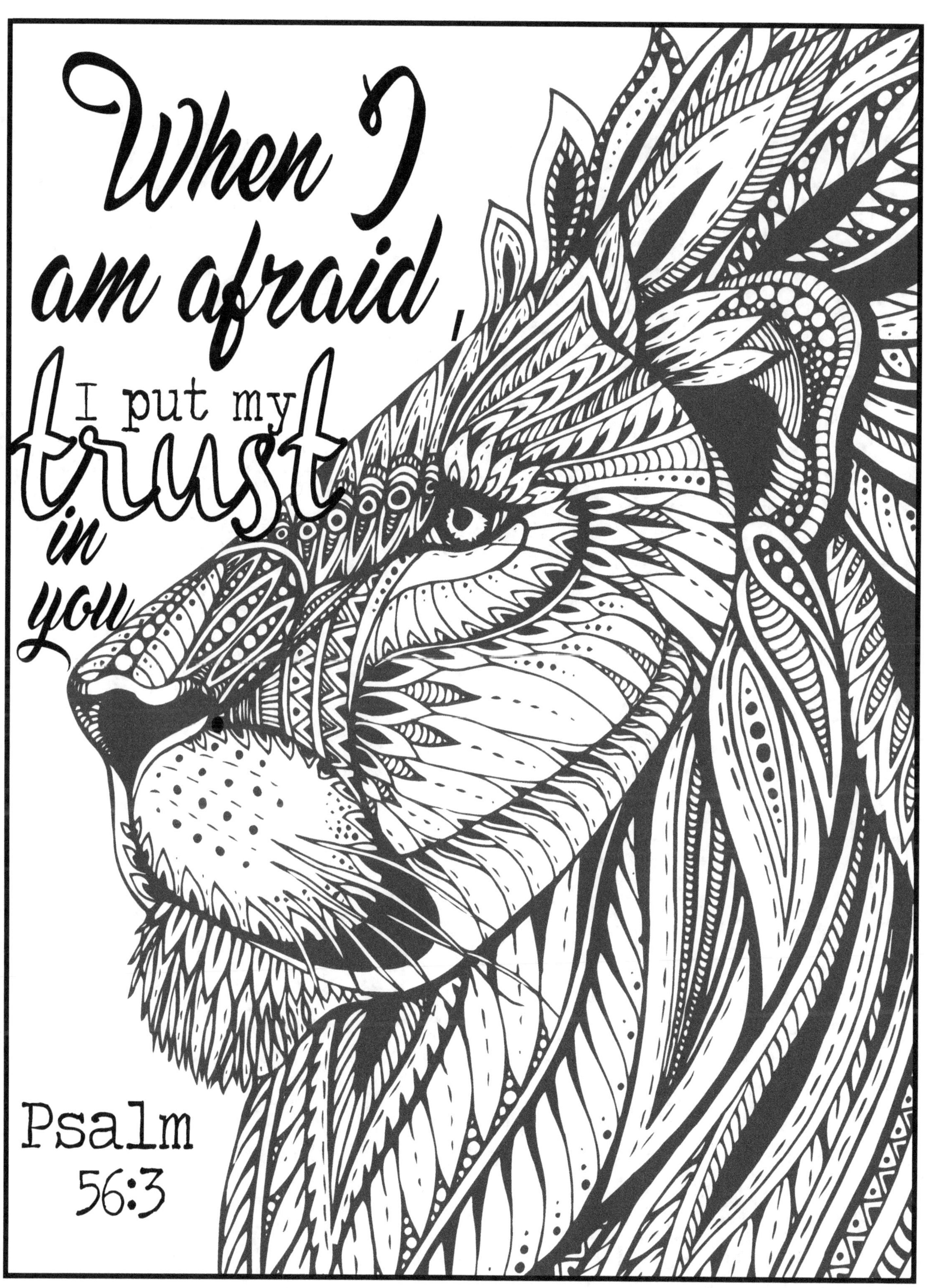

When I am afraid,
I put my
trust
in you
Psalm
56:3

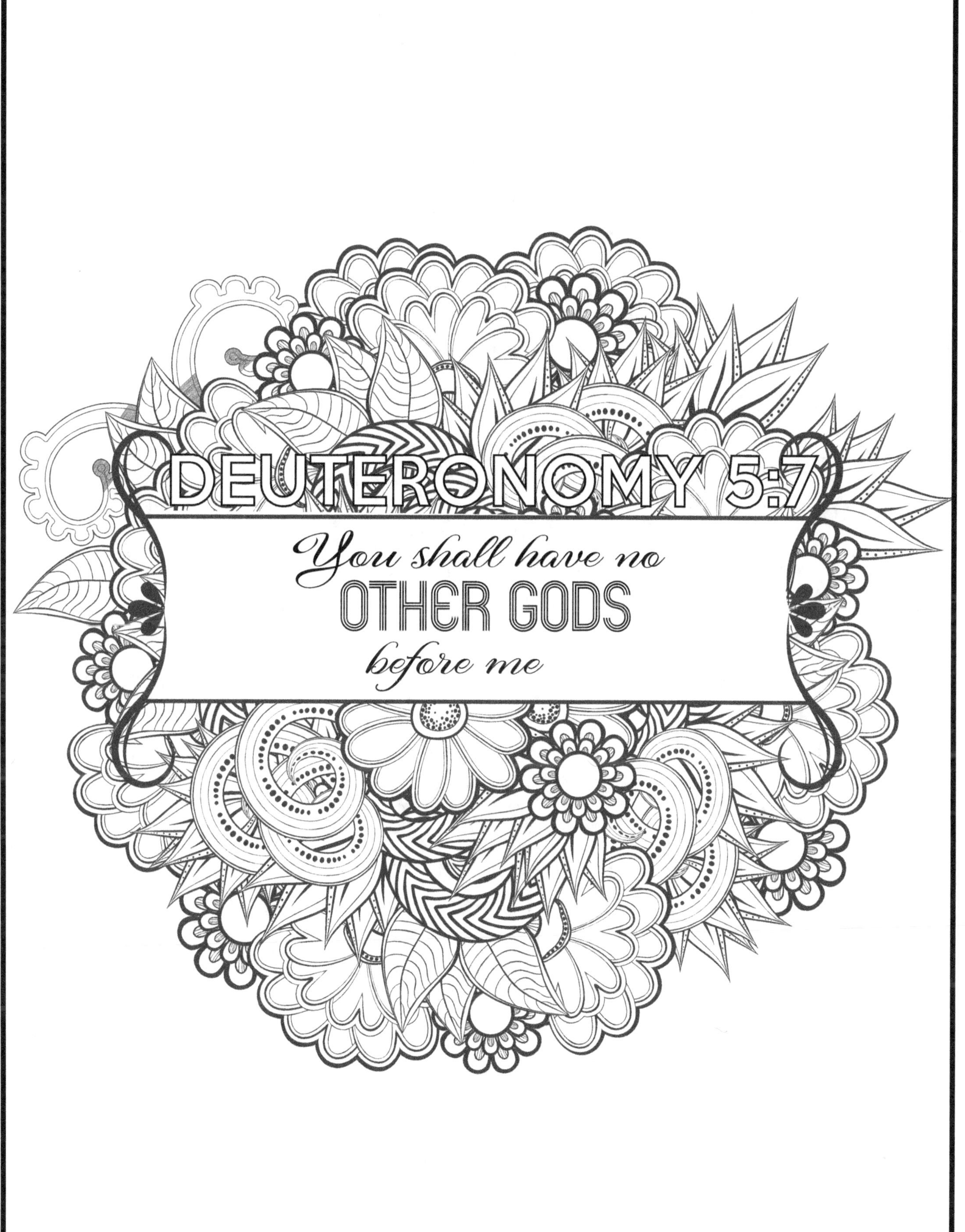
DEUTERONOMY 5:7
You shall have no
OTHER GODS
before me

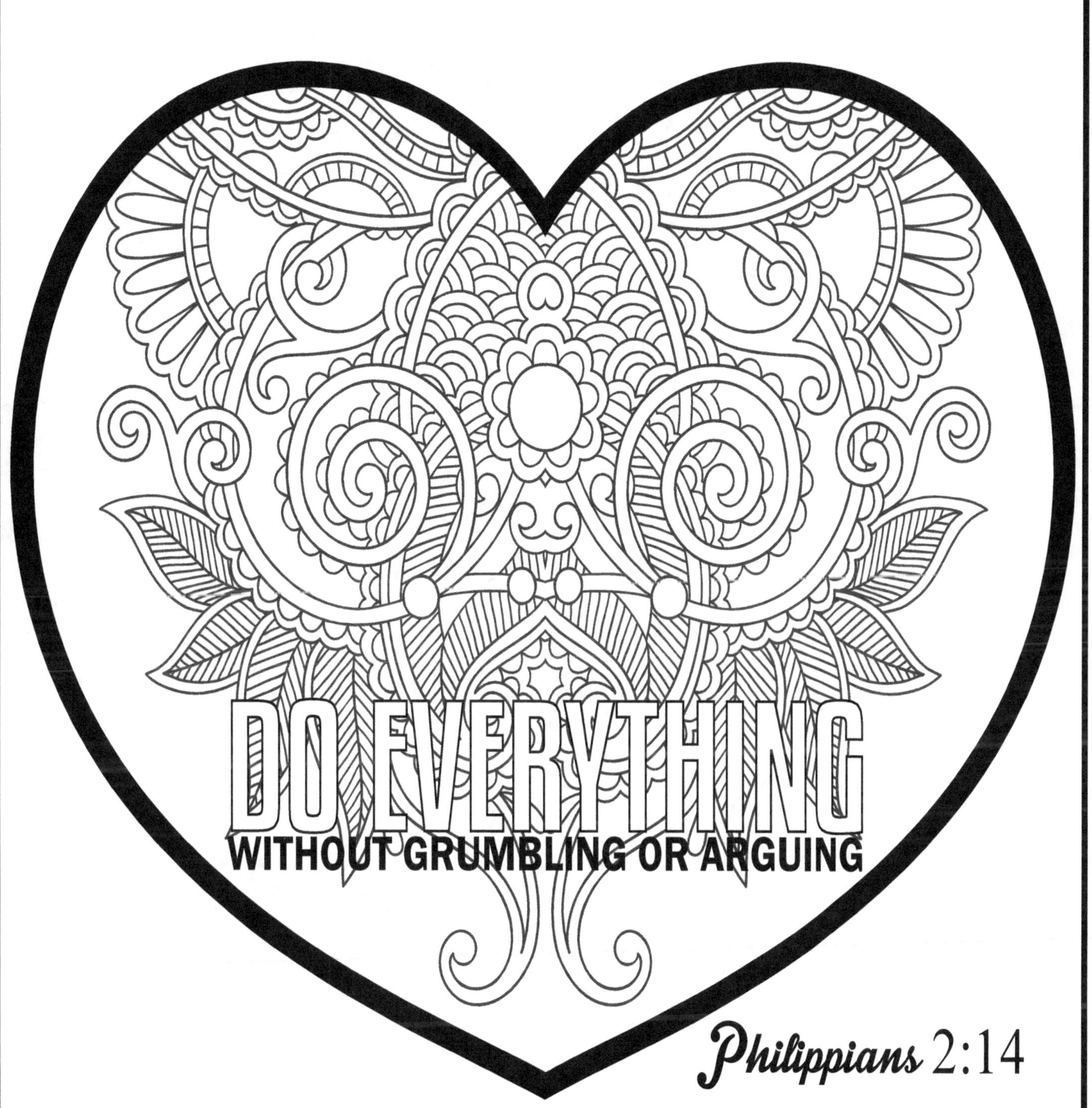

DO EVERYTHING
WITHOUT GRUMBLING OR ARGUING
Philippians 2:14

But Godliness with contentment is great gain.

1 Timothy 6:6

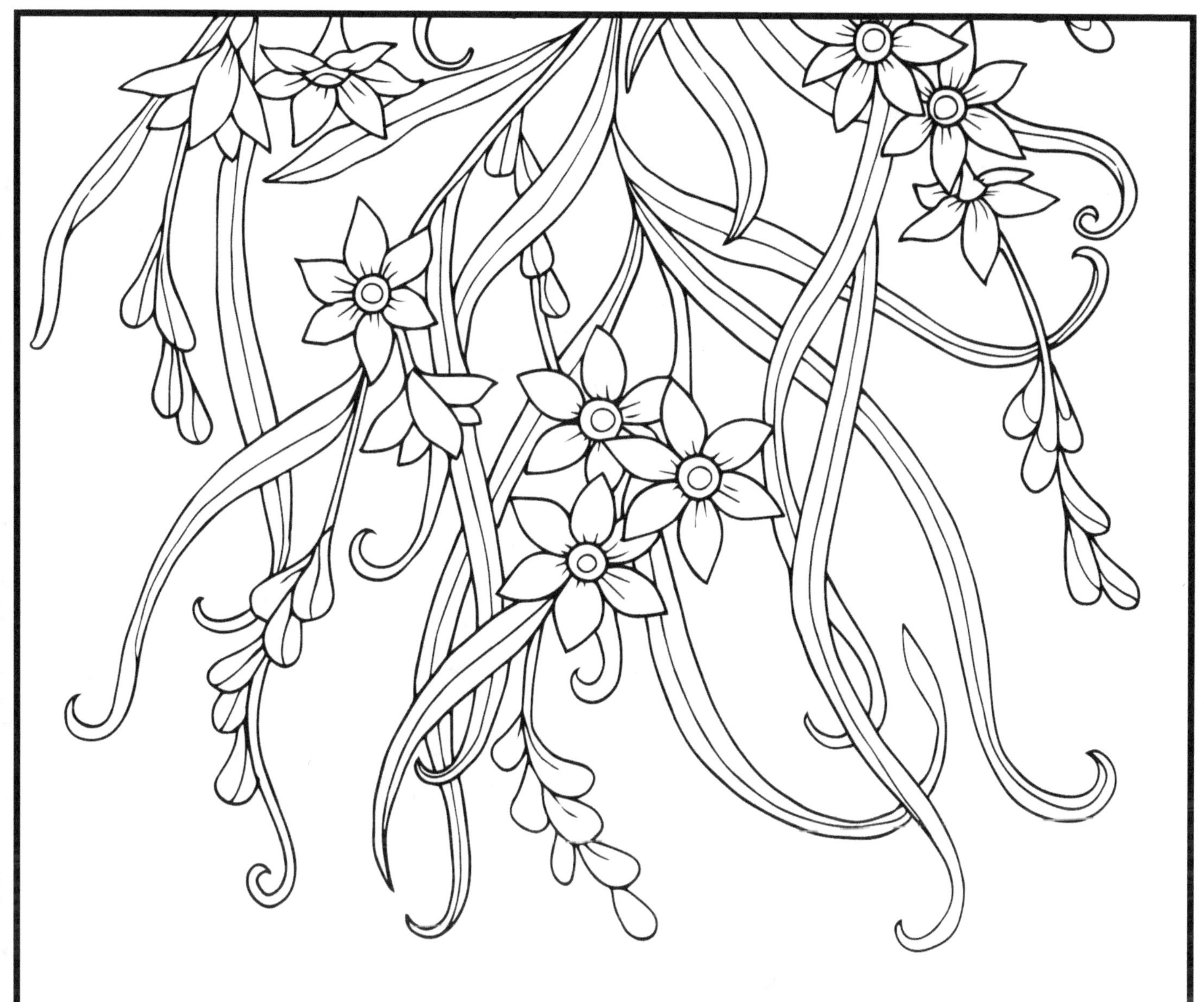

because he **loves** our nation and has built our synagogue

Luke 7:5

The LORD
gives strength to his people;

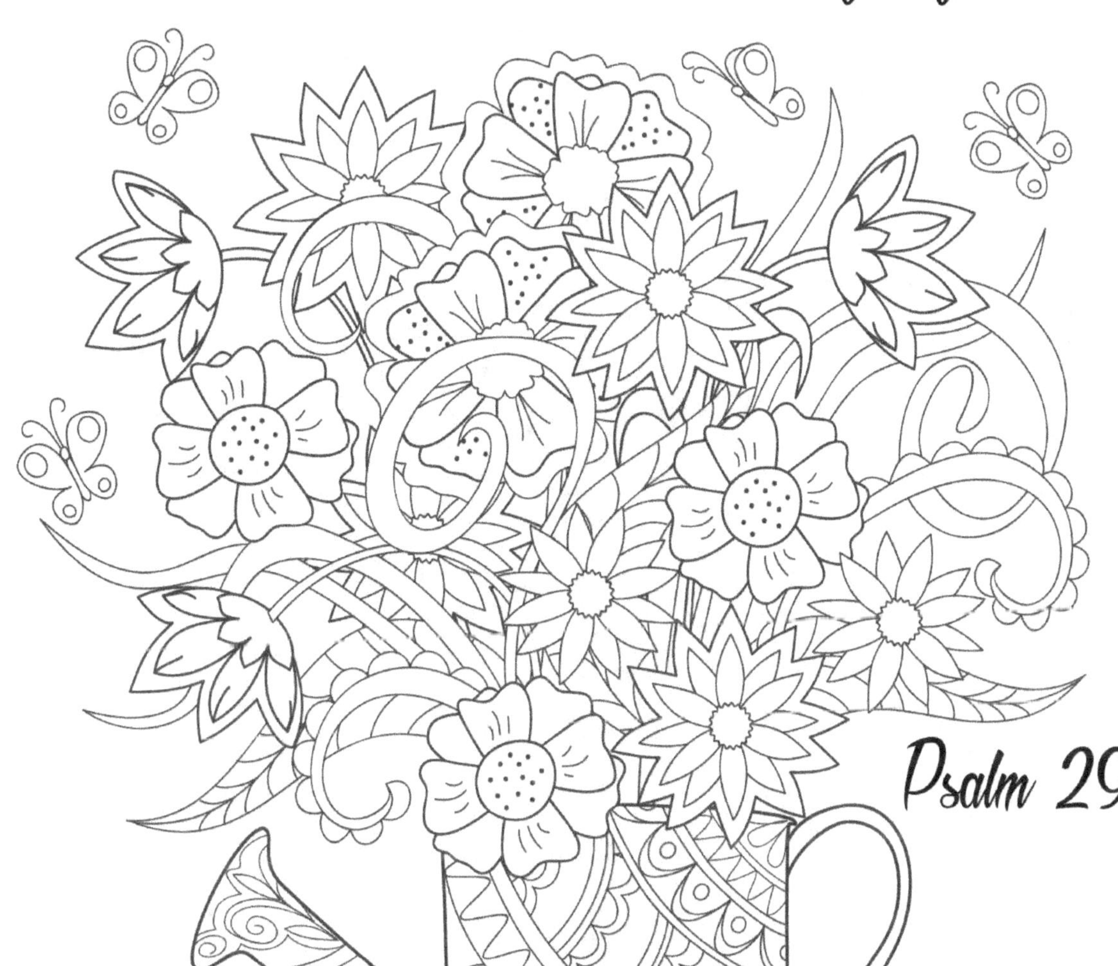

Psalm 29:11

The LORD
blesses his people with peace.

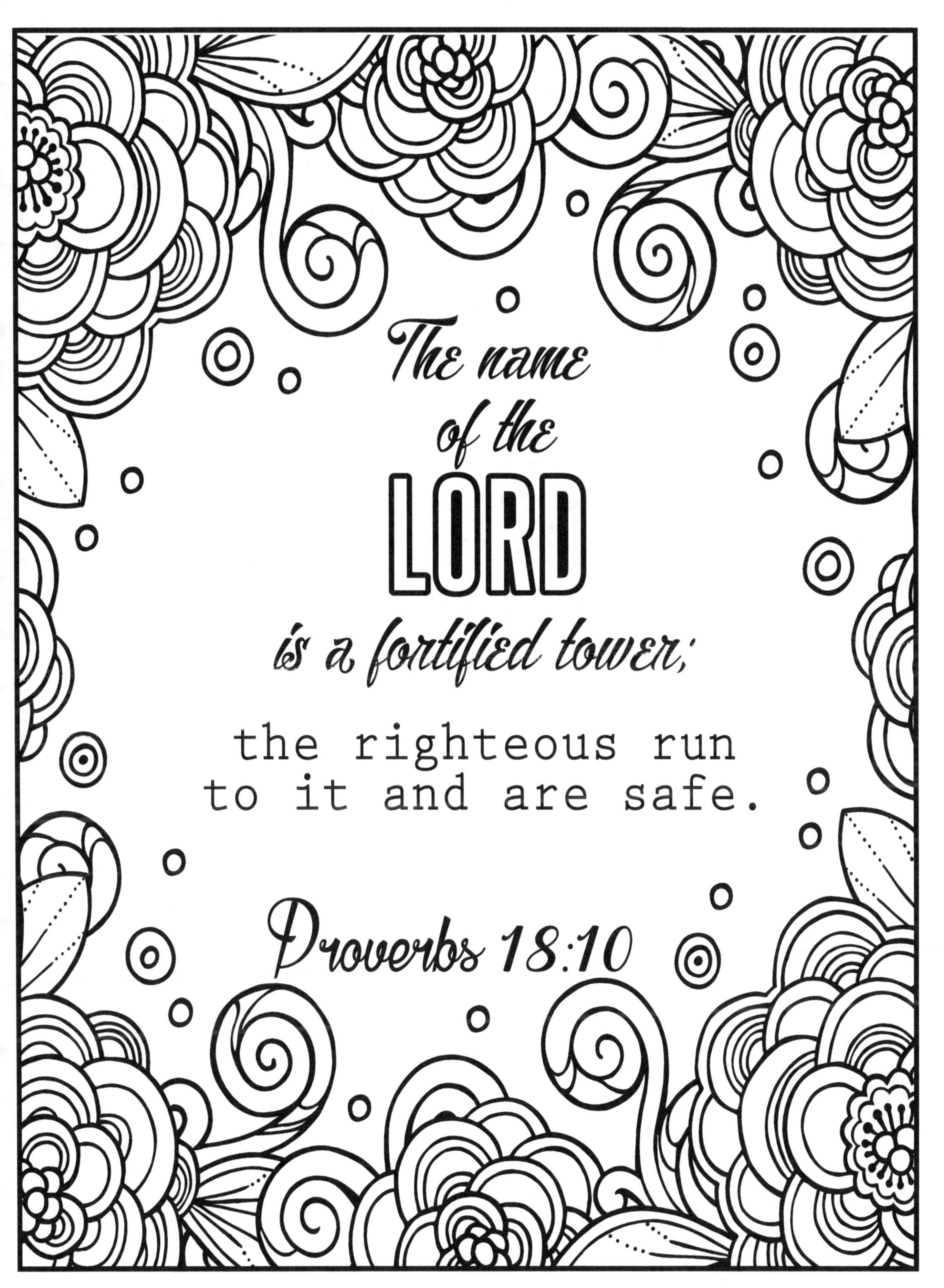

The name
of the
LORD
is a fortified tower;
the righteous run
to it and are safe.
Proverbs 18:10

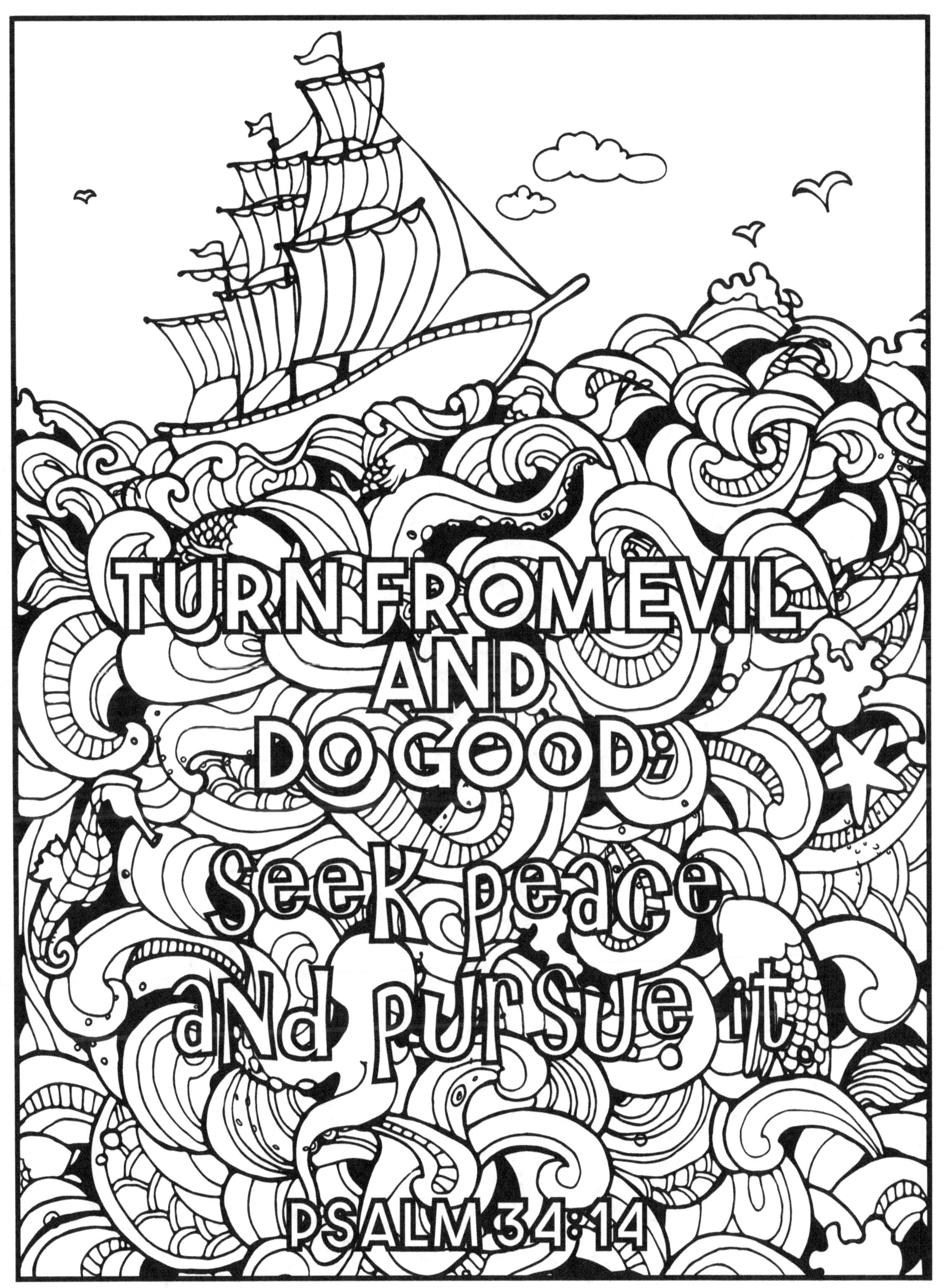

TURN FROM EVIL
AND
DO GOOD;
Seek peace
and pursue it
PSALM 34:14

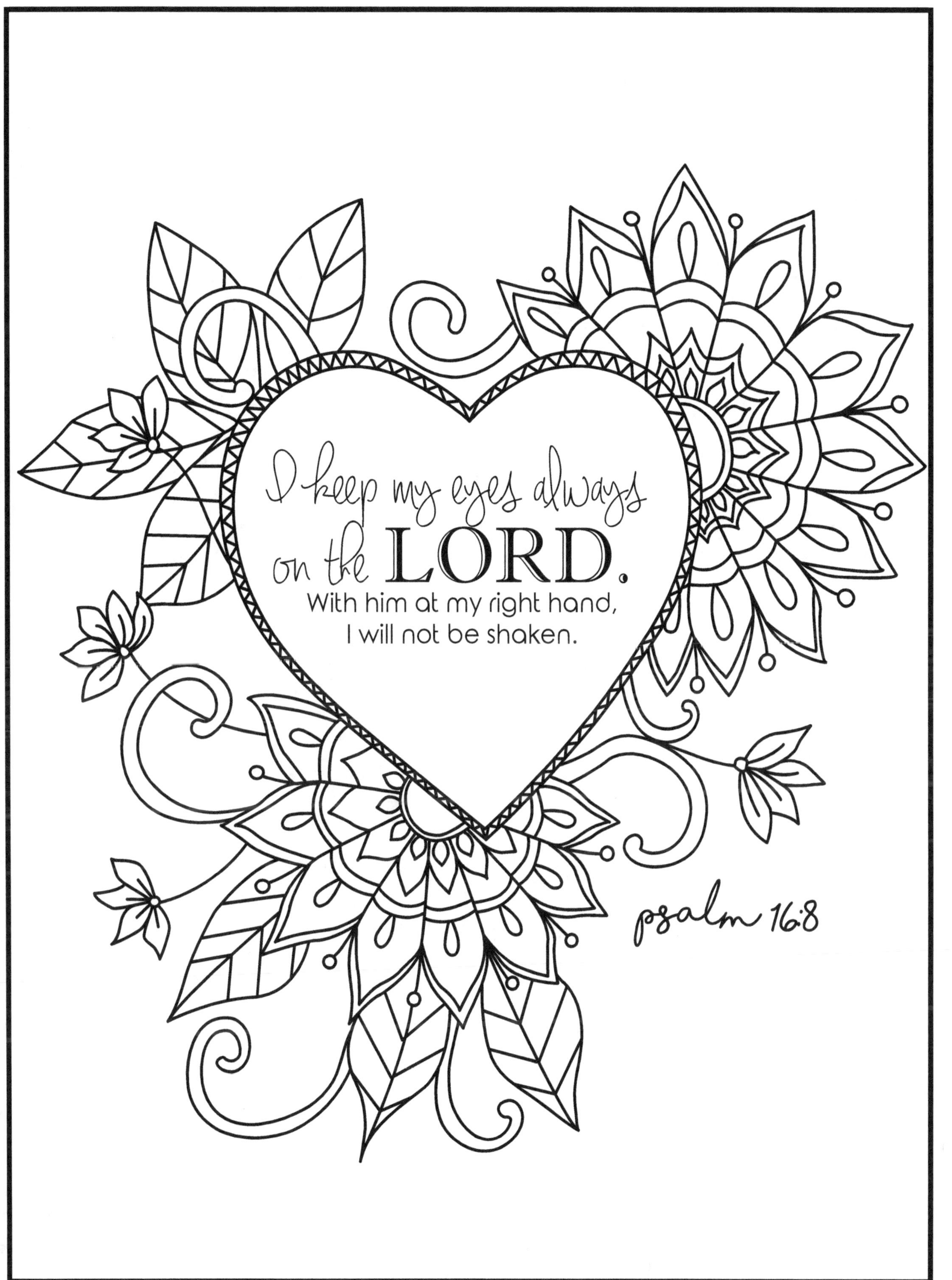

I keep my eyes always
on the LORD.
With him at my right hand,
I will not be shaken.
psalm 16:8

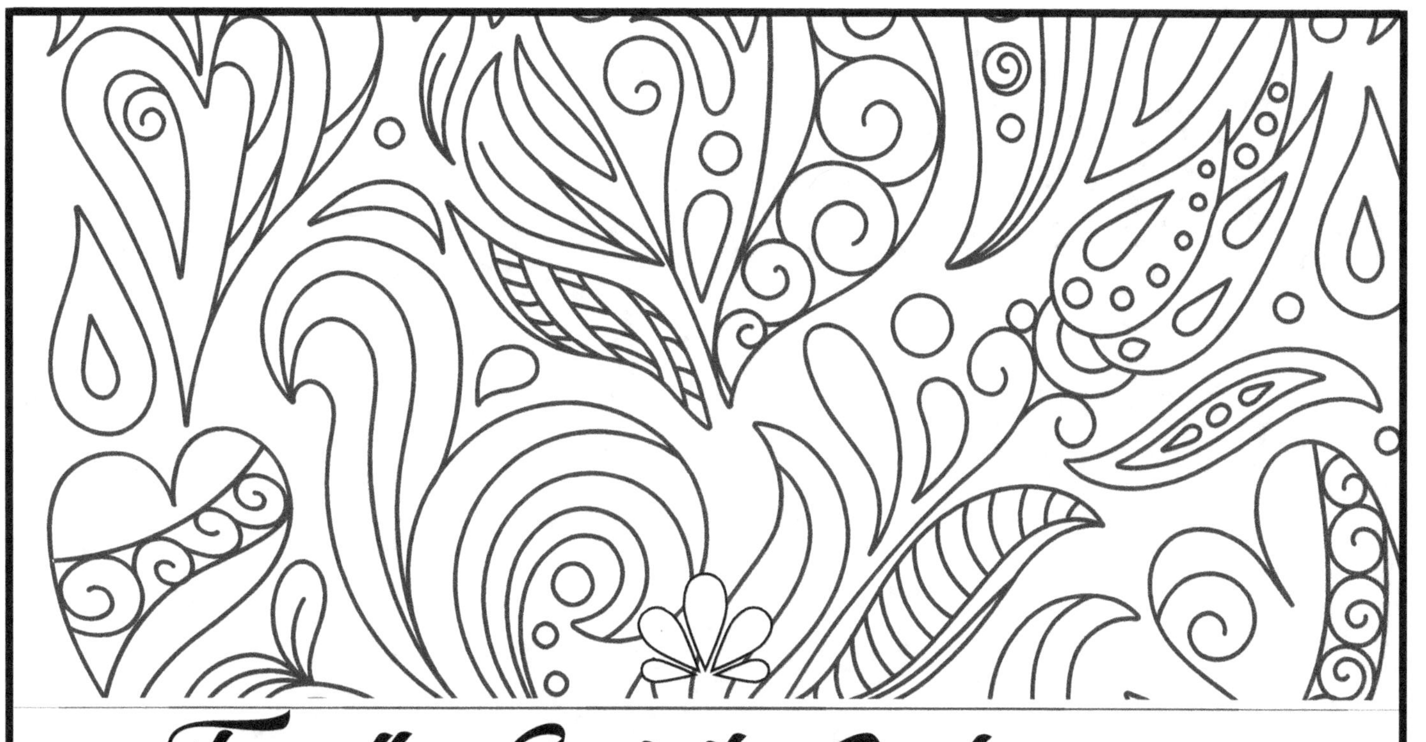

For the Spirit God gave us does not make us timid,
but gives us power, love and self-discipline.
2 Timothy 1:7

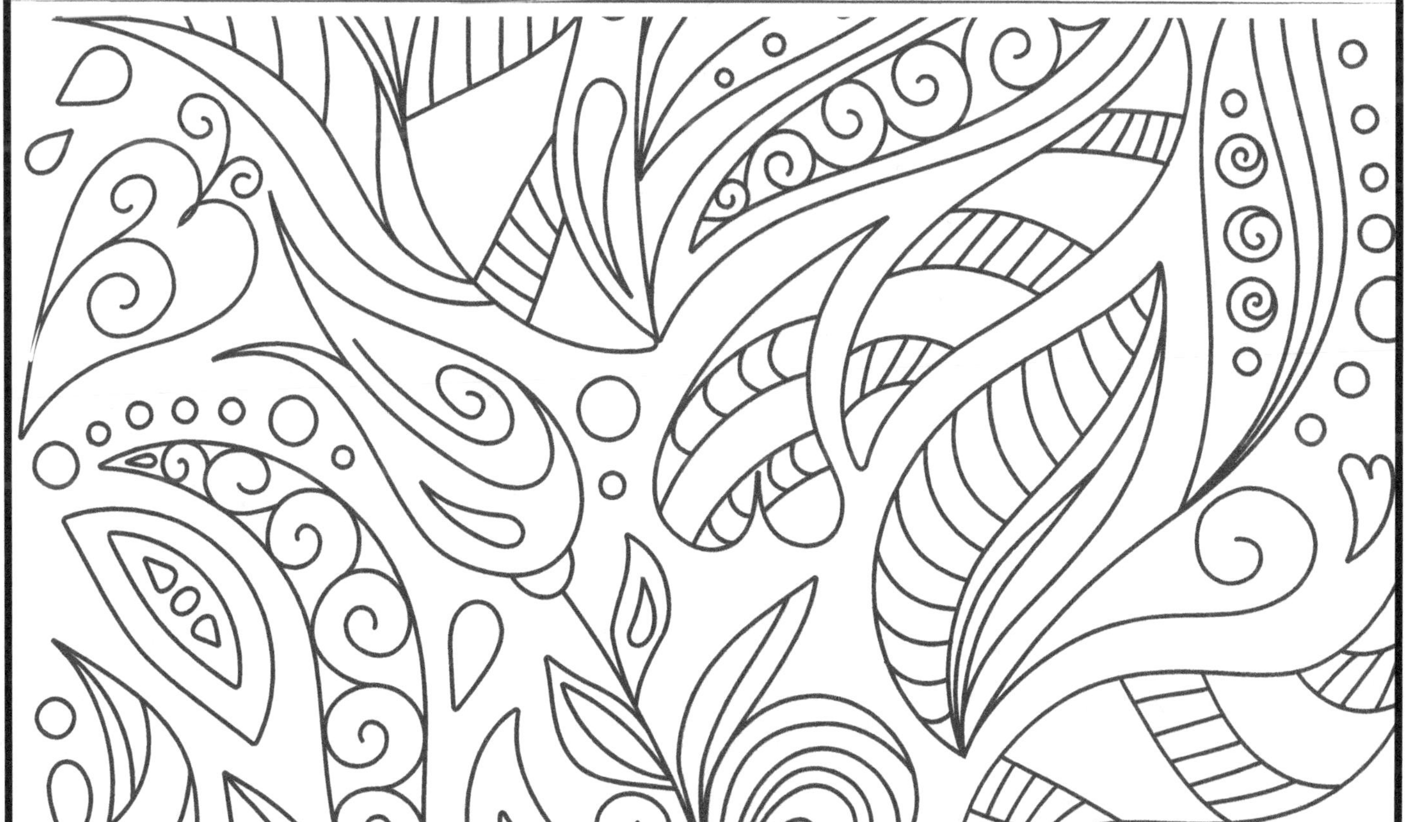

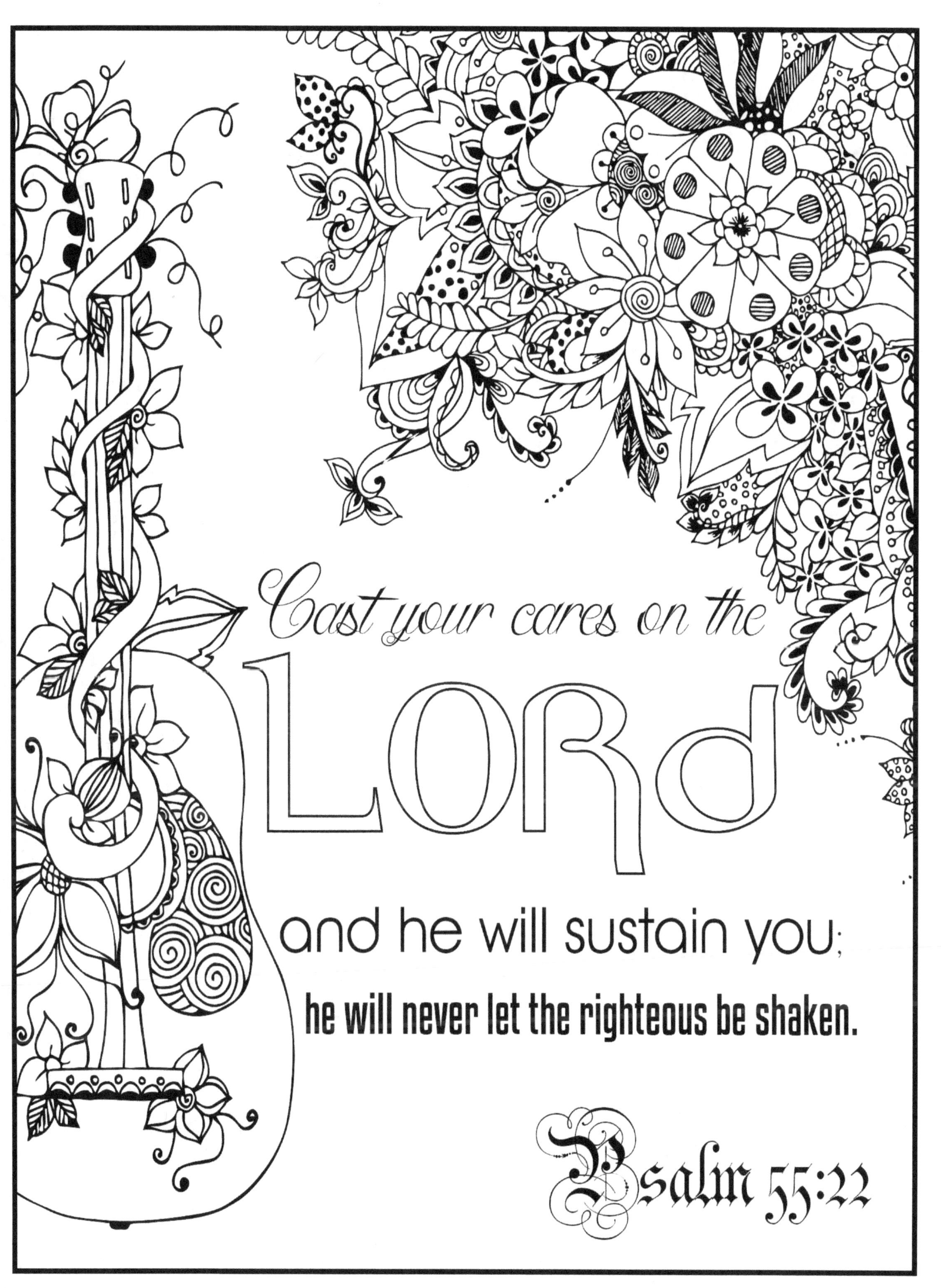

Cast your cares on the
LORd
and he will sustain you;
he will never let the righteous be shaken.
Psalm 55:22

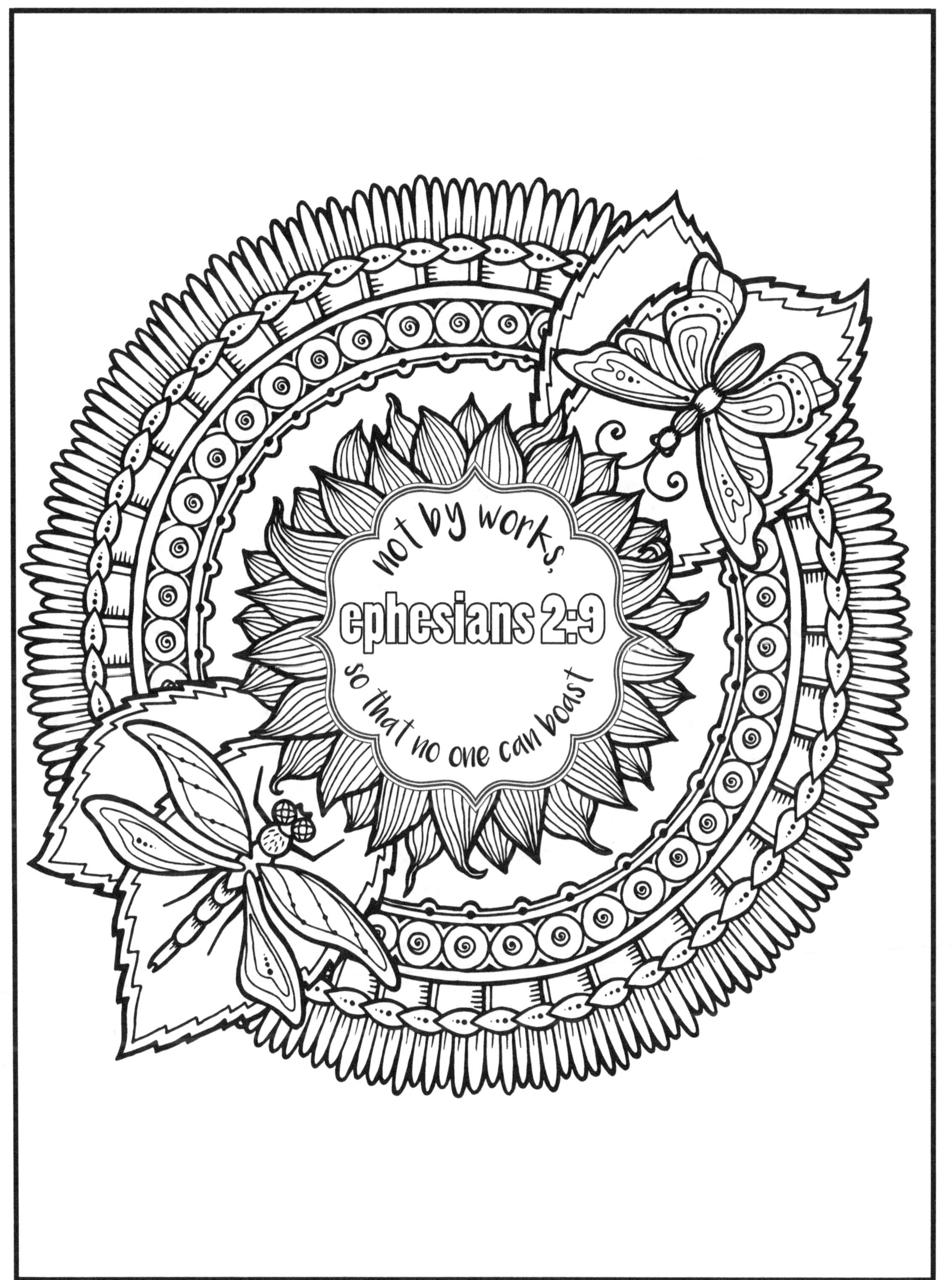

not by works,
ephesians 2:9
so that no one can boast

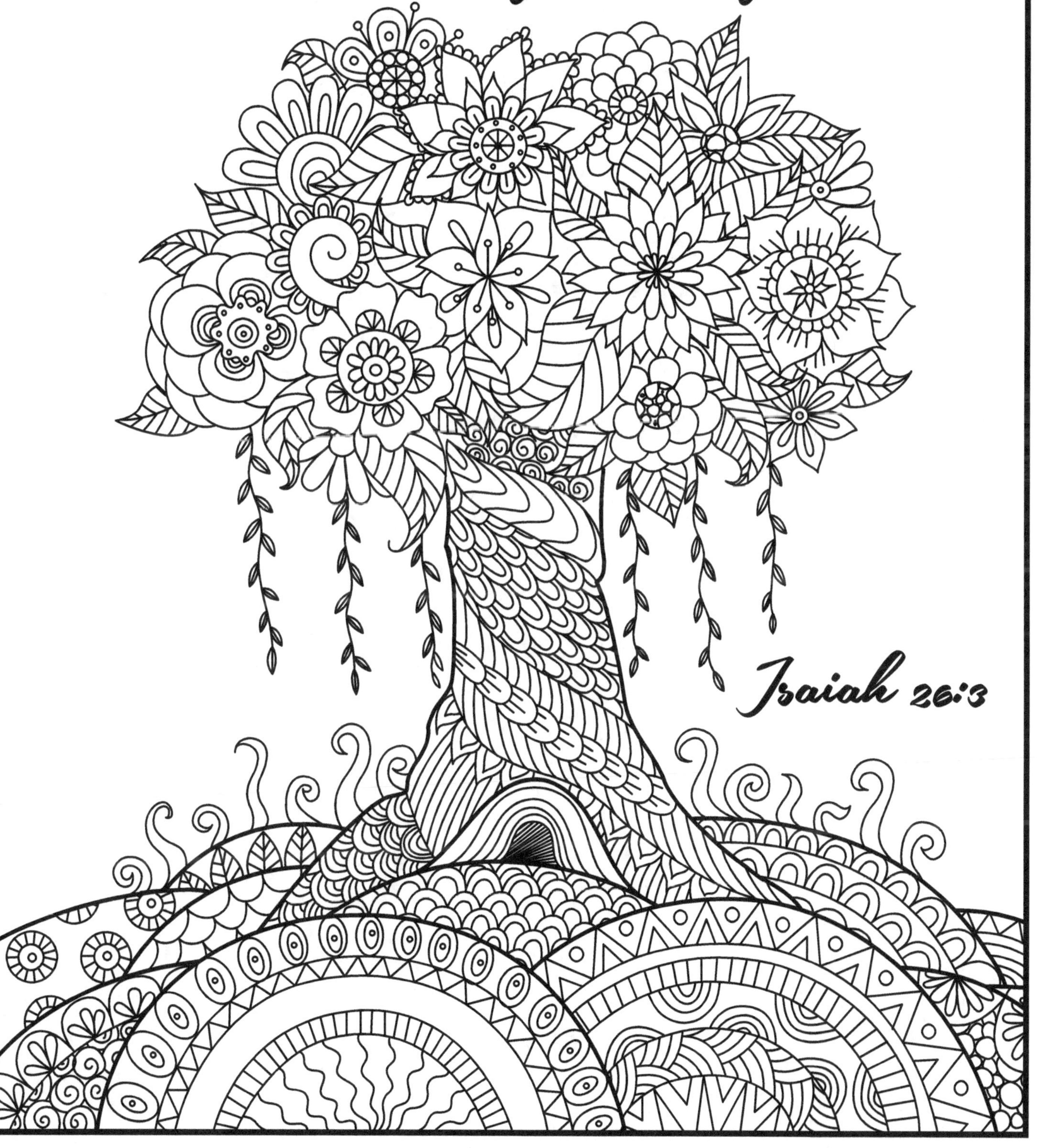
You will keep in perfect peace
those whose minds are steadfast,
because they trust in you.

Isaiah 26:3

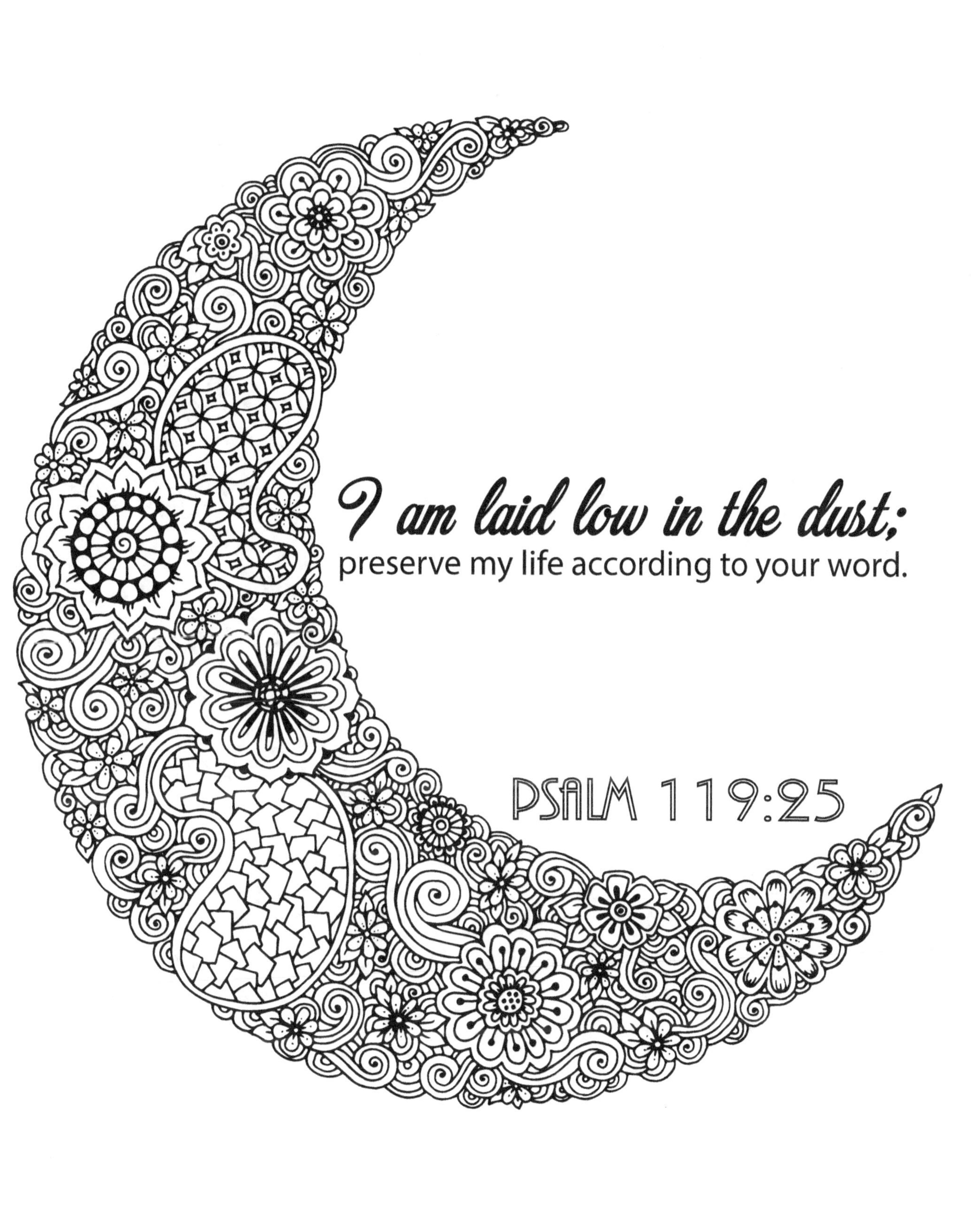

I am laid low in the dust;
preserve my life according to your word.
PSALM 119:25

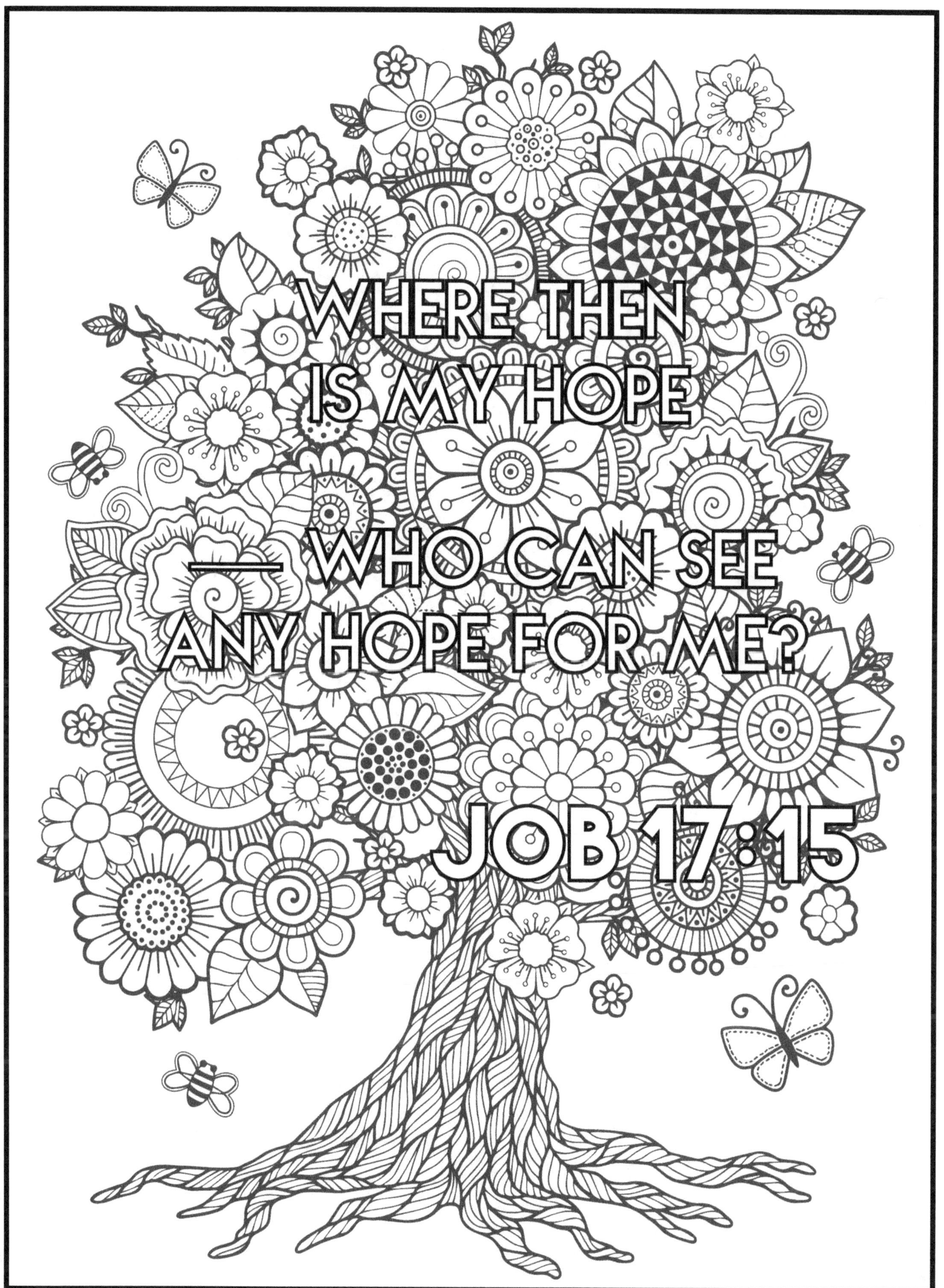
WHERE THEN IS MY HOPE
— WHO CAN SEE ANY HOPE FOR ME?
JOB 17:15

SO THE POOR HAVE HOPE,

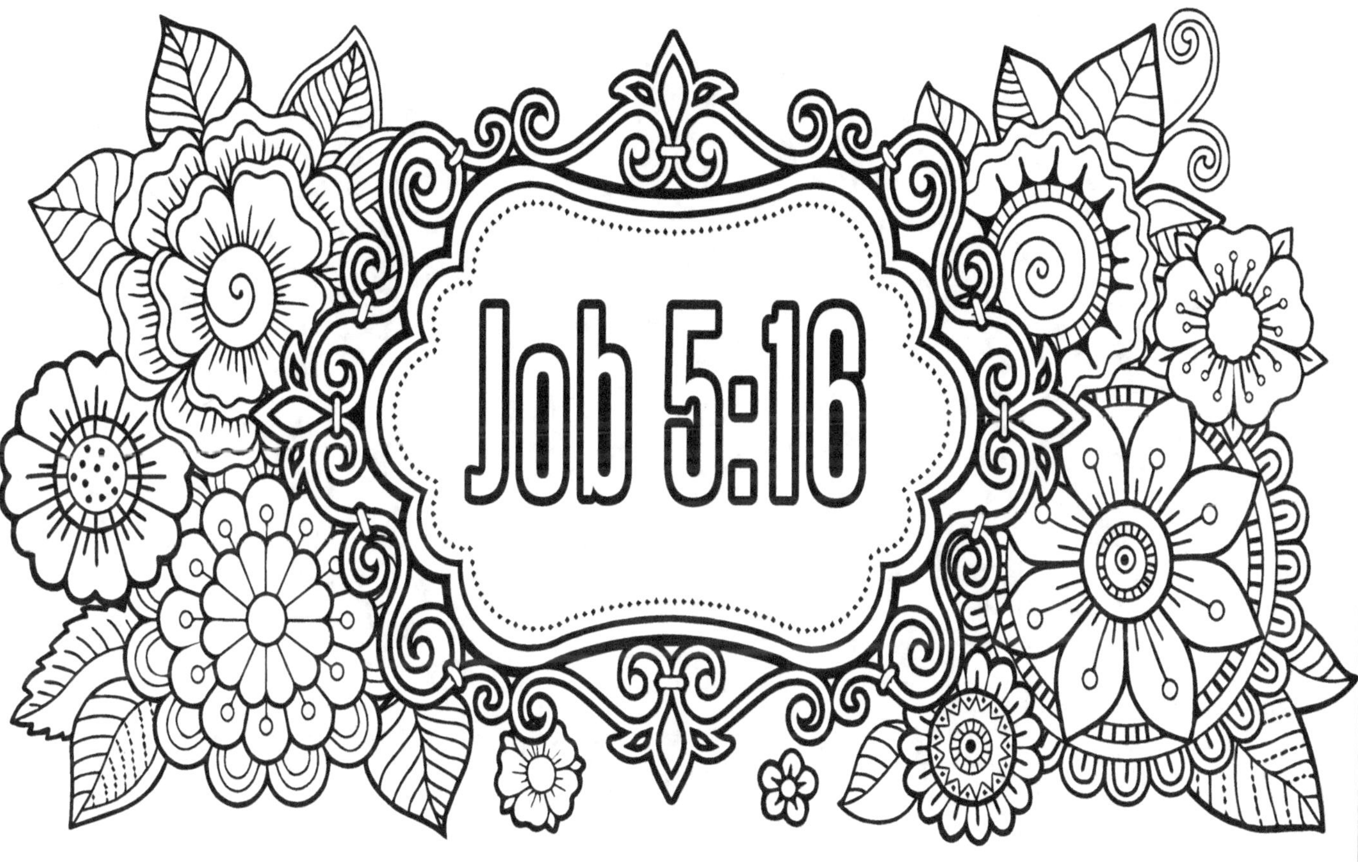

AND IN
JUSTICE SHUTS ITS MOUTH.

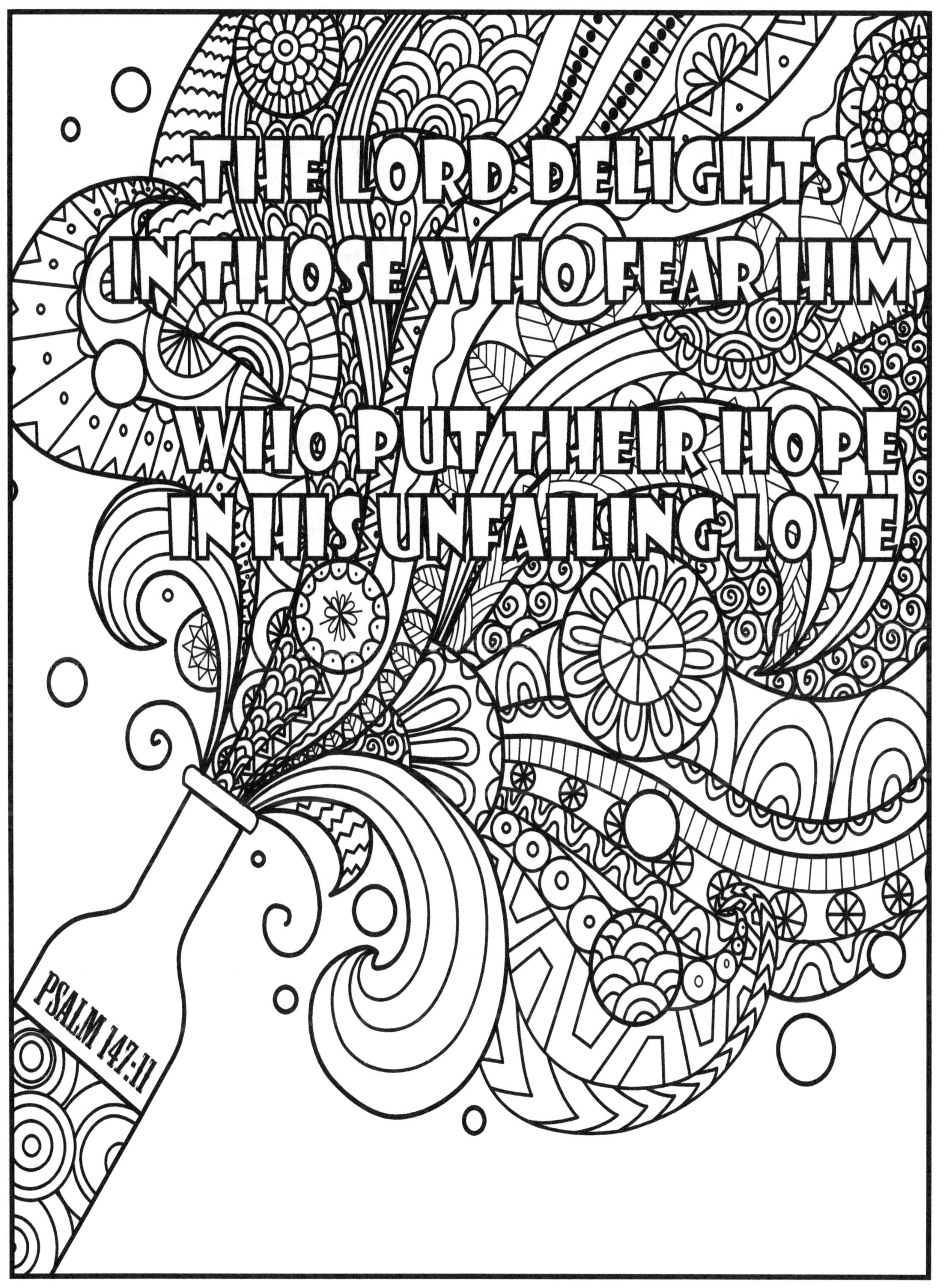

THE LORD DELIGHTS
IN THOSE WHO FEAR HIM
WHO PUT THEIR HOPE
IN HIS UNFAILING LOVE.
PSALM 147:11

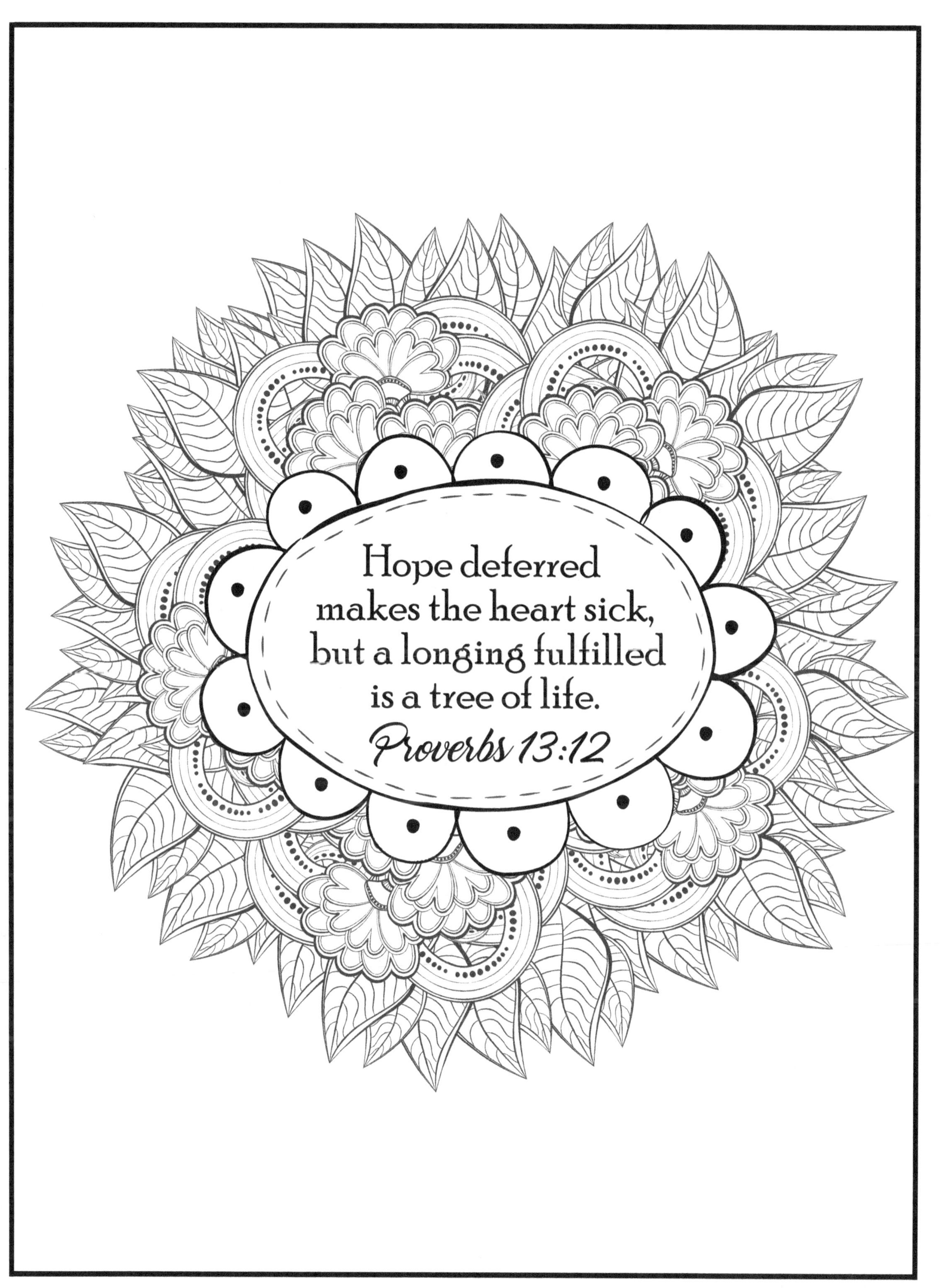
Hope deferred
makes the heart sick,
but a longing fulfilled
is a tree of life.
Proverbs 13:12

Walk with the wise and become wise,

for a companion of fools suffers harm.

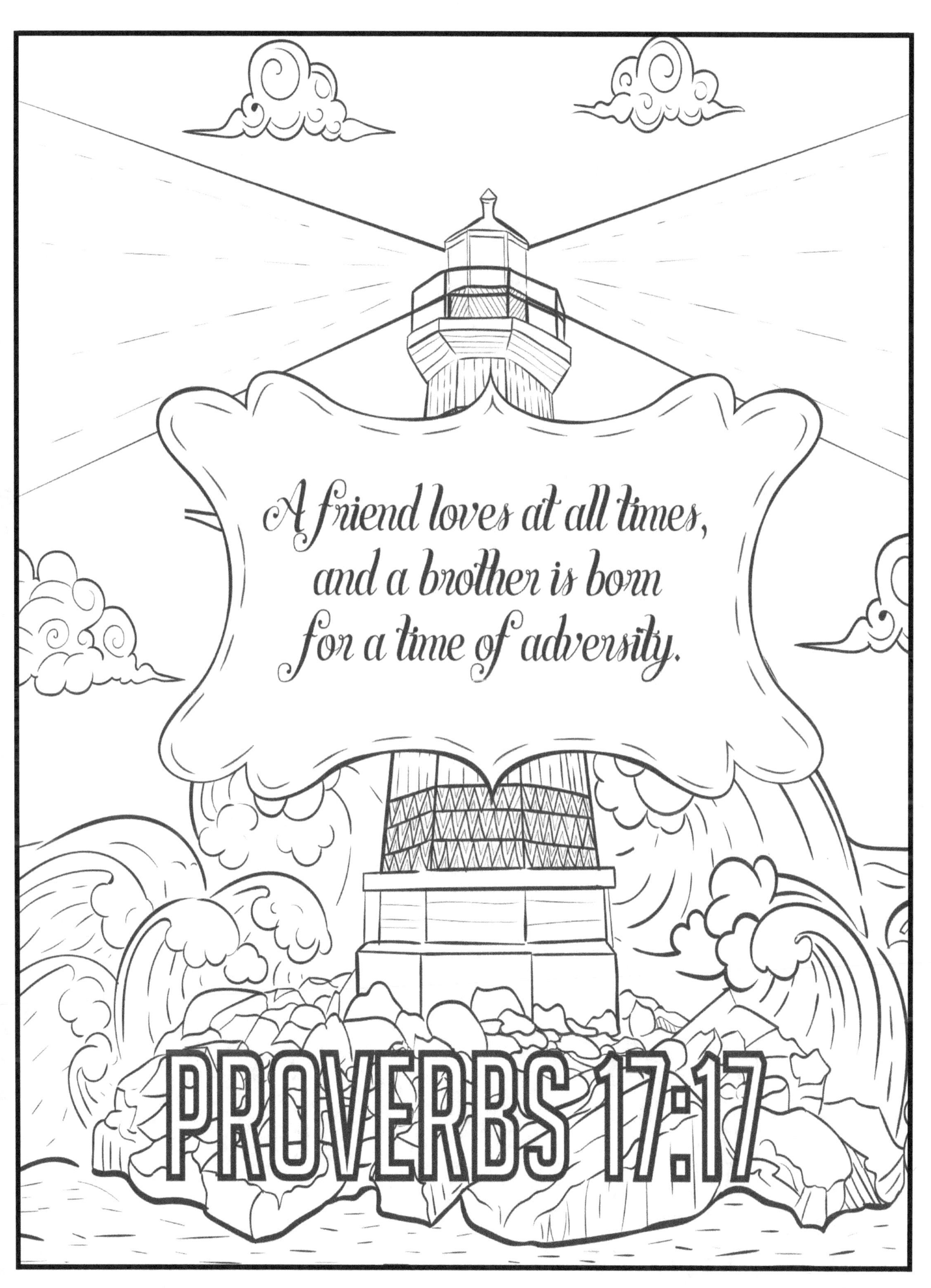

A friend loves at all times,
and a brother is born
for a time of adversity.
PROVERBS 17:17

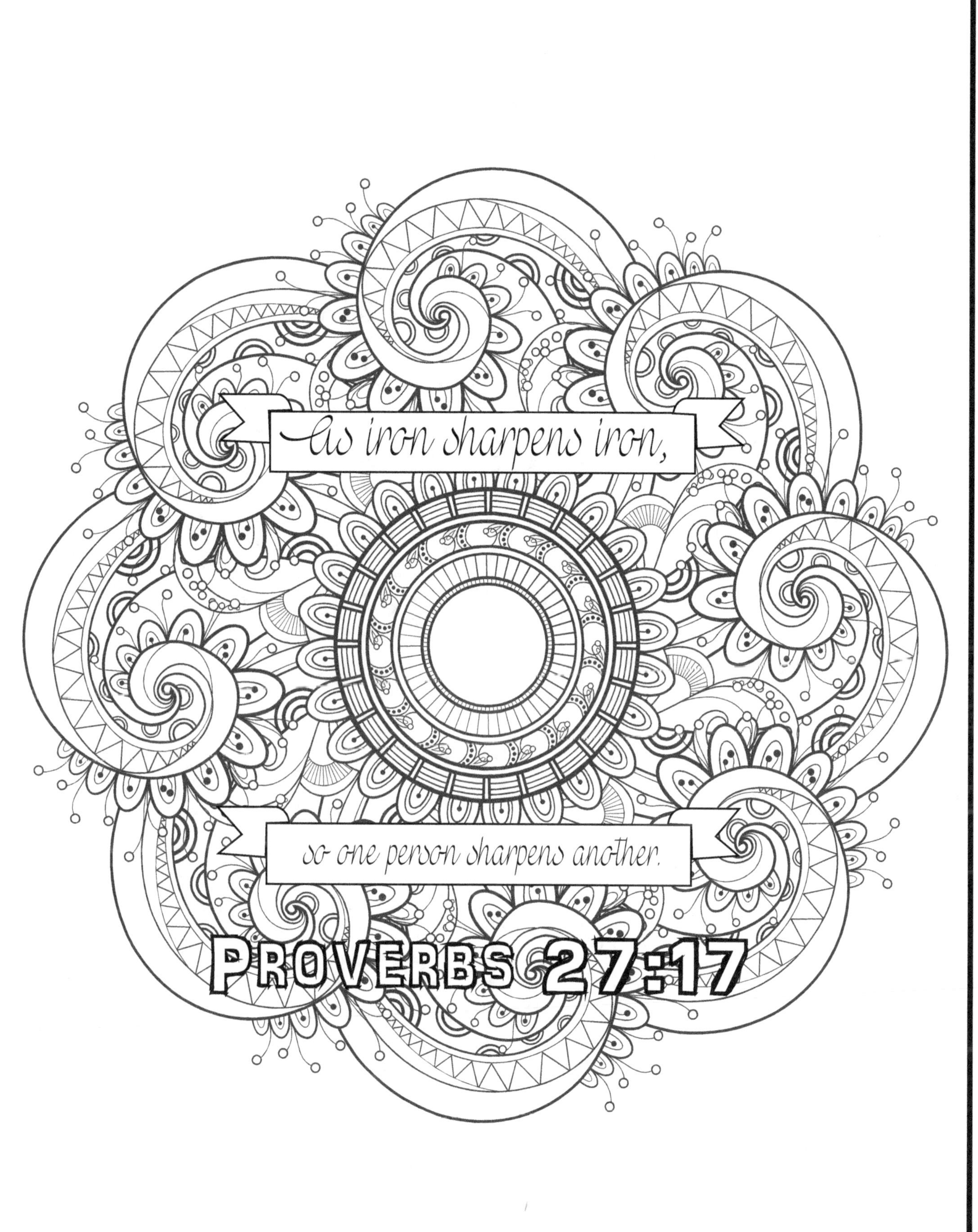
As iron sharpens iron,
so one person sharpens another.
PROVERBS 27:17

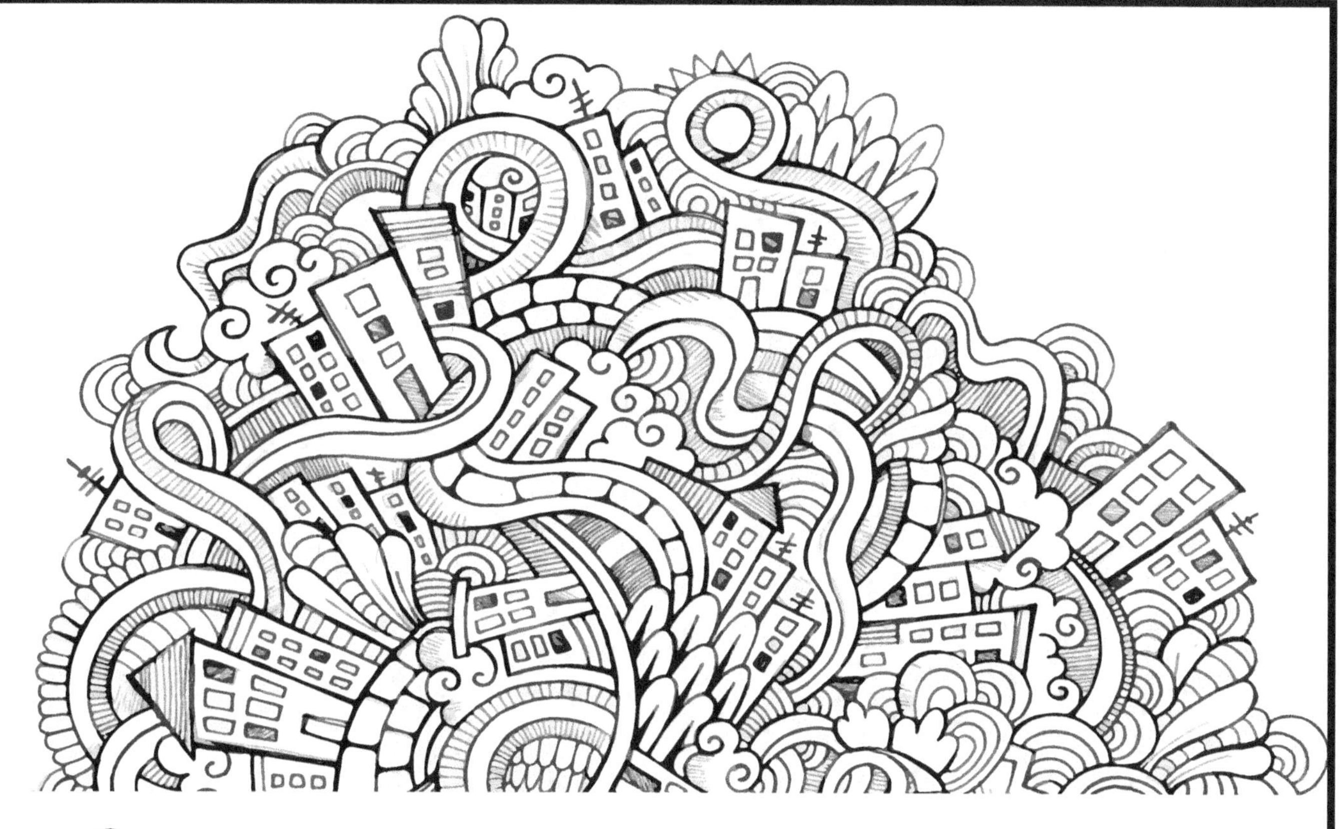

Look to the LORD and his strength;
seek his face always.

1 CHRONICLES 16:11

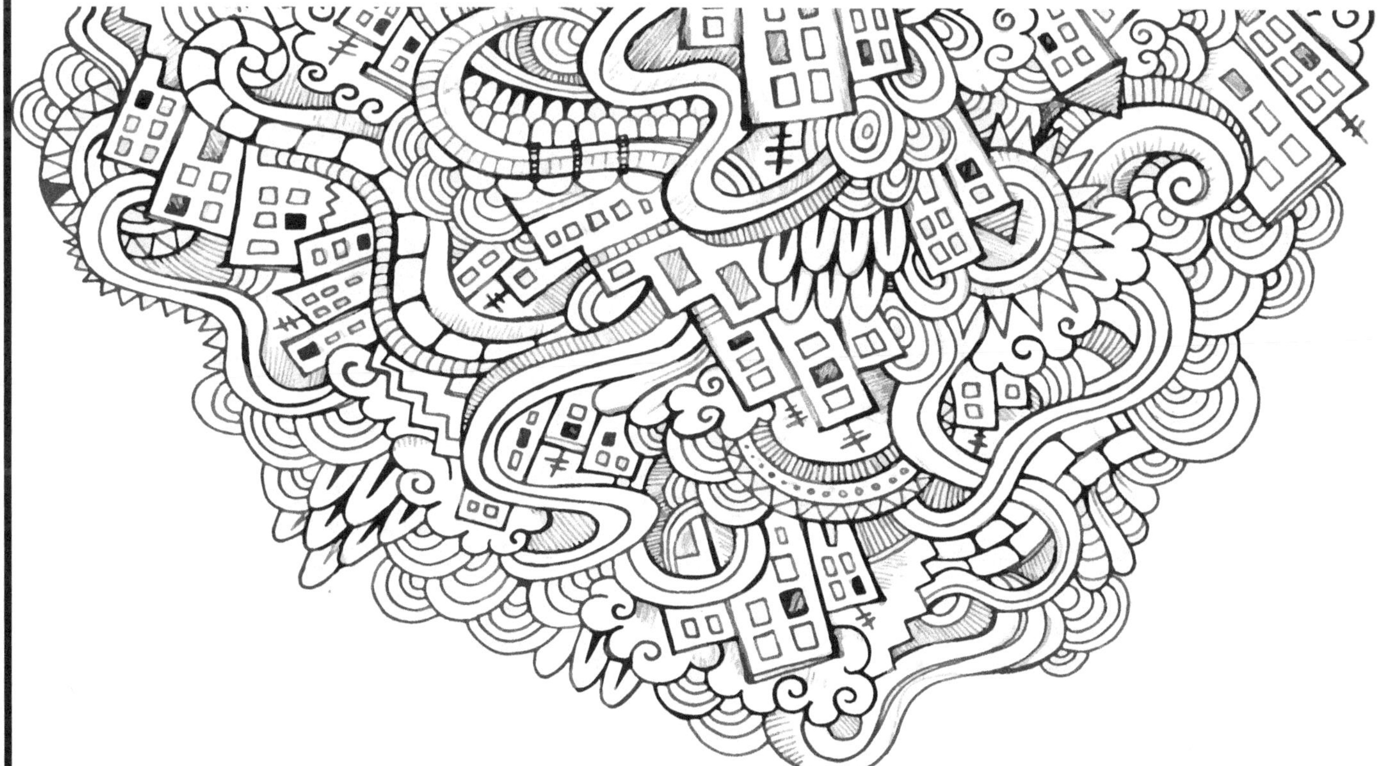

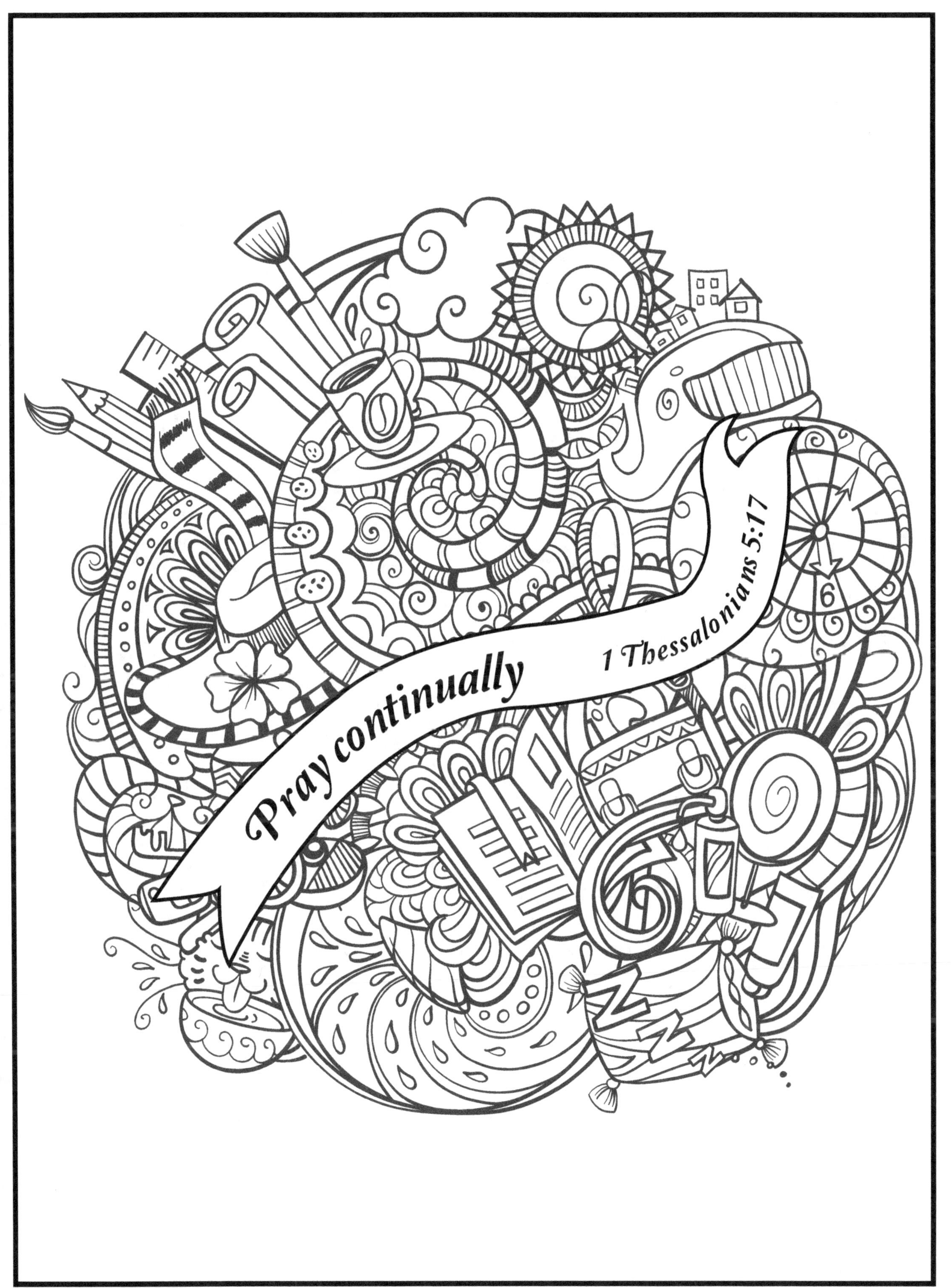

Pray continually
1 Thessalonians 5:17

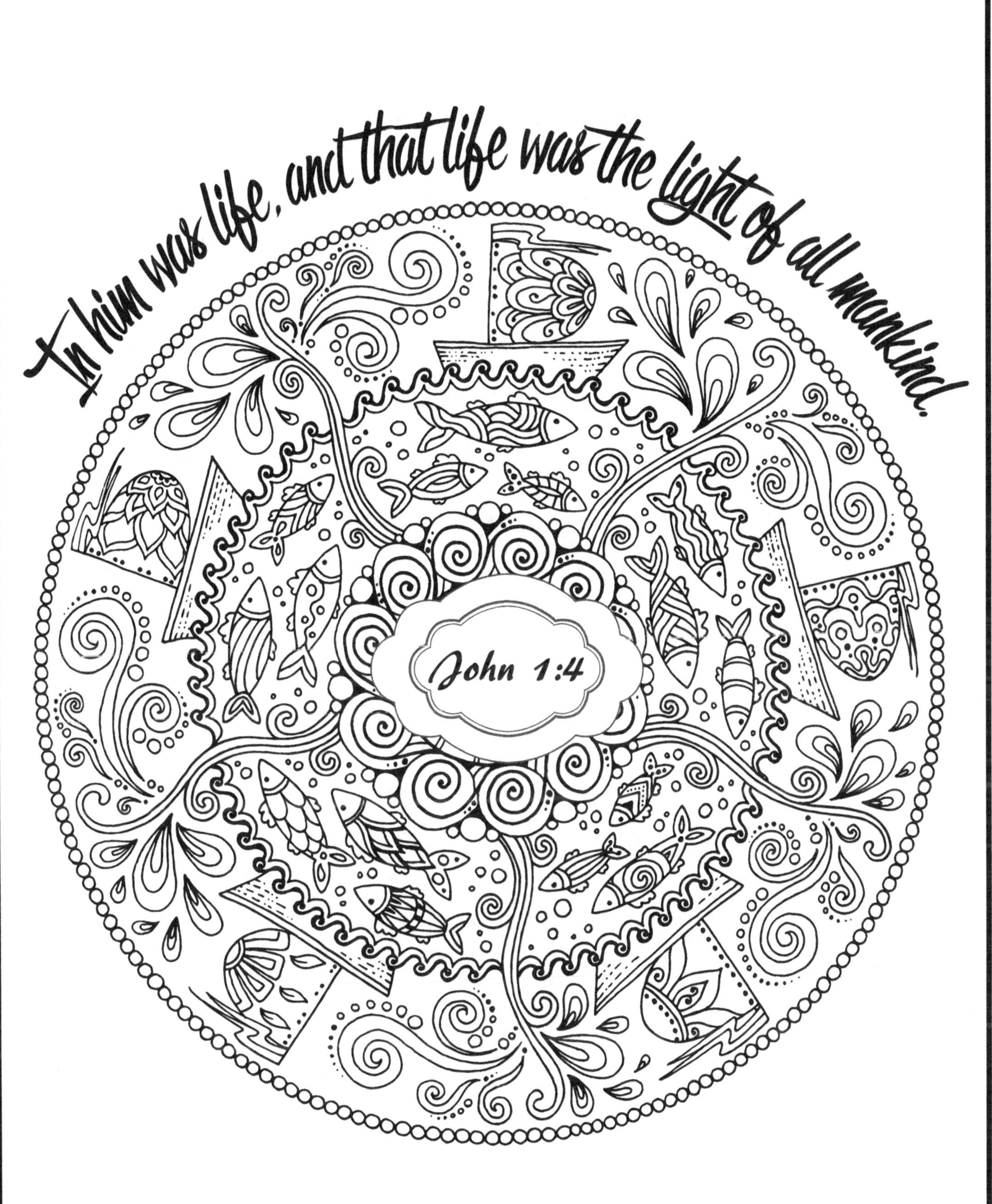

In him was life, and that life was the light of all mankind.
John 1:4

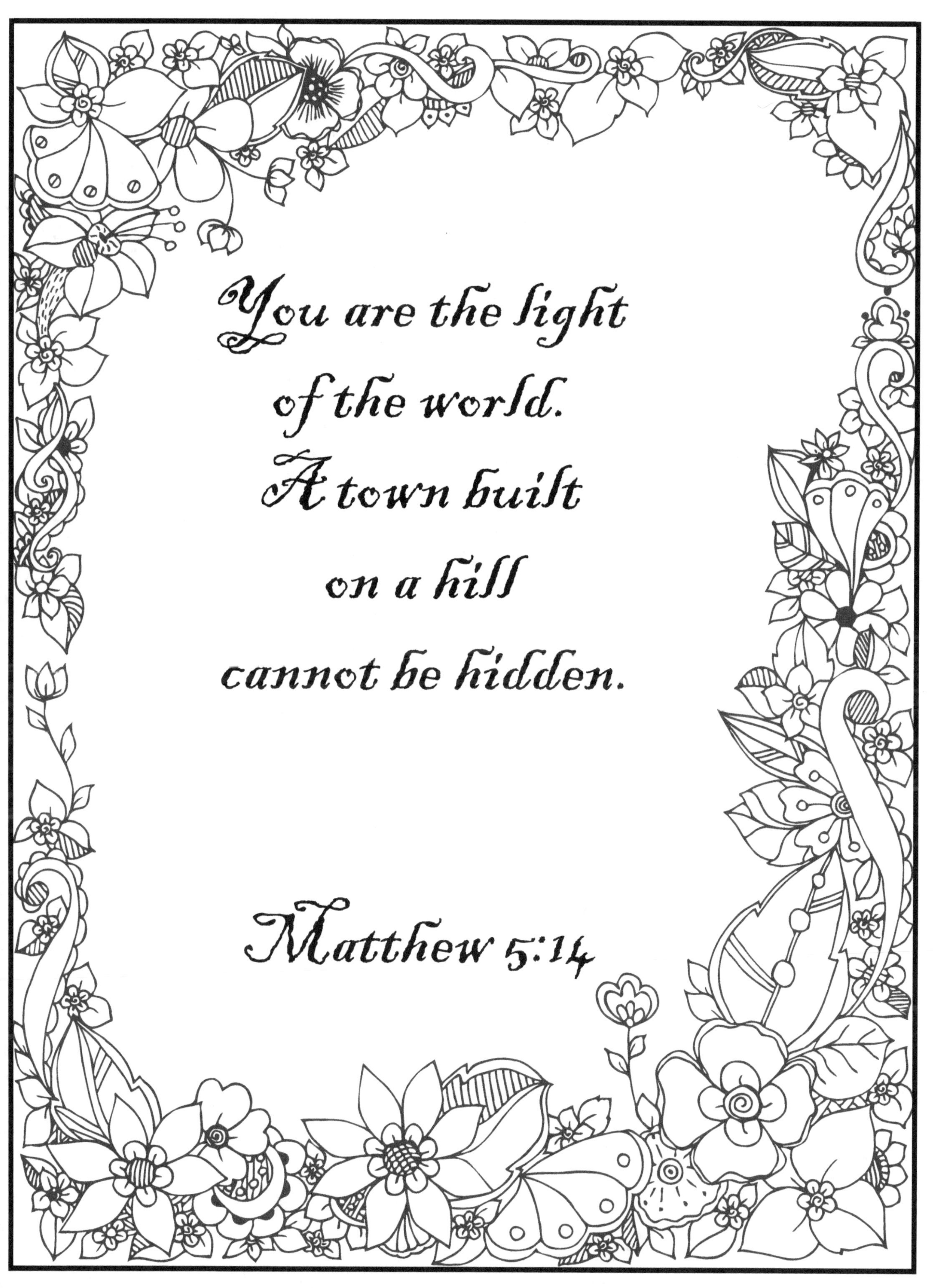

You are the light
of the world.
A town built
on a hill
cannot be hidden.

Matthew 5:14

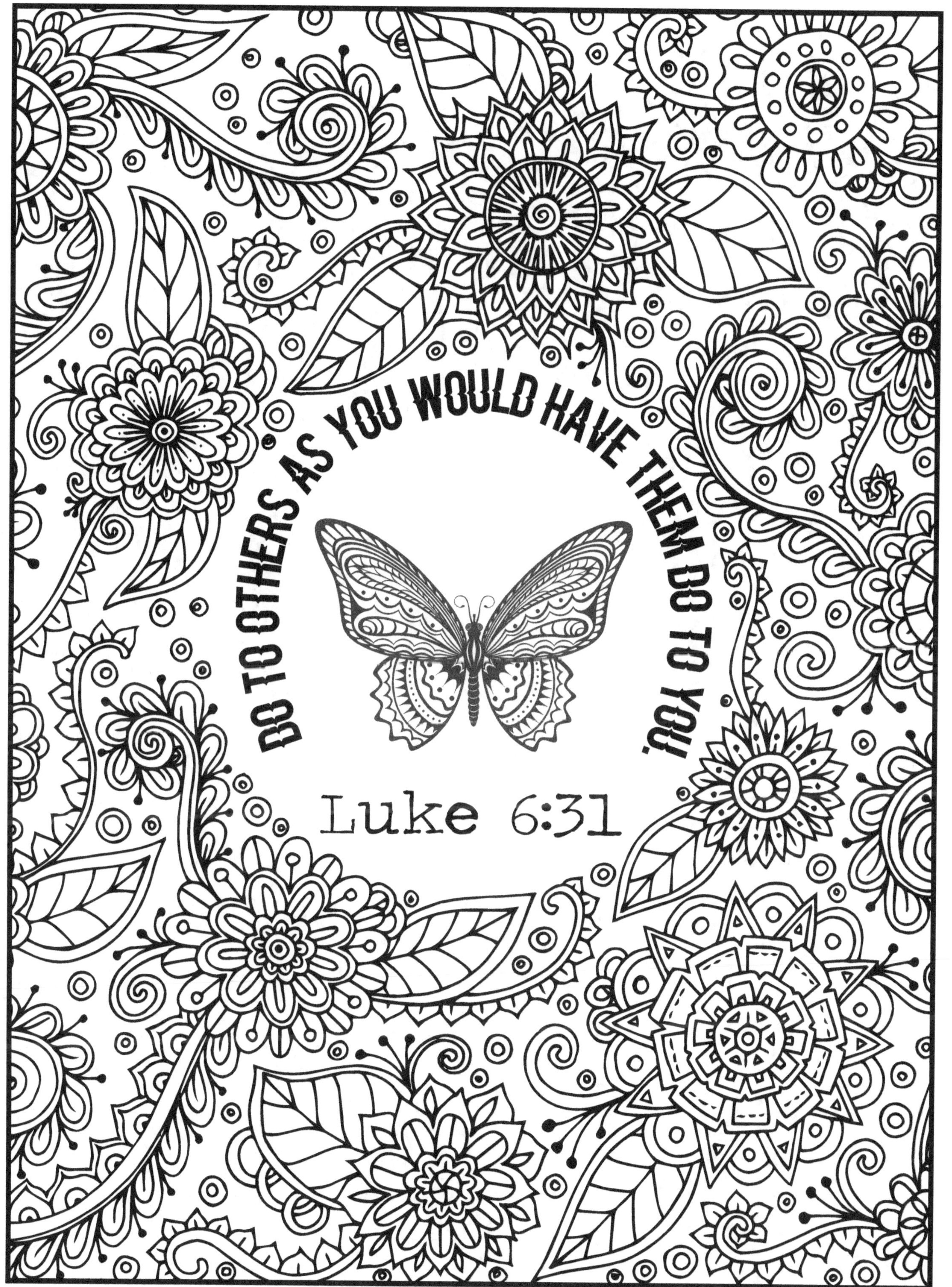

DO TO OTHERS AS YOU WOULD HAVE THEM DO TO YOU.
Luke 6:31

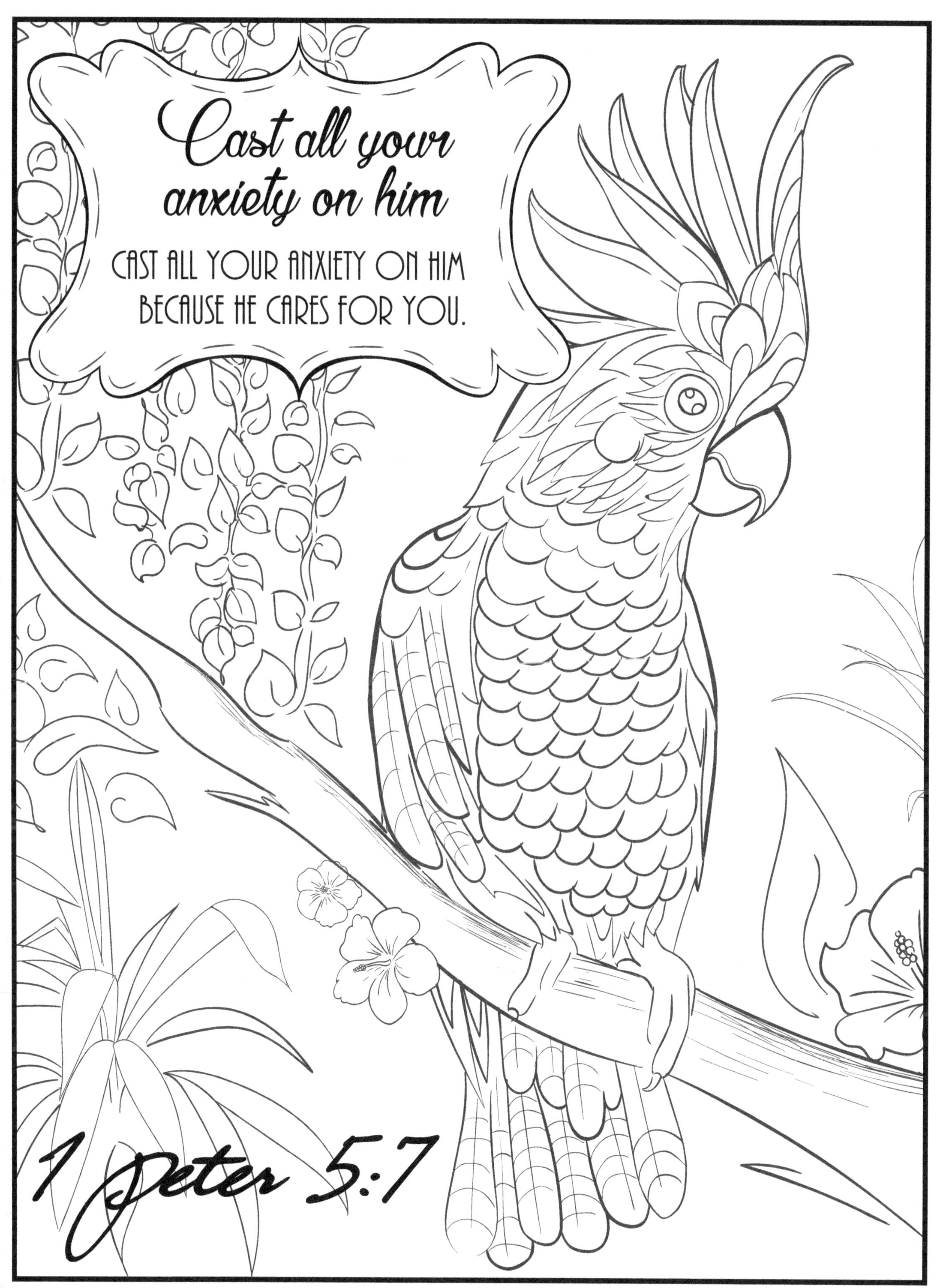
Cast all your anxiety on him
CAST ALL YOUR ANXIETY ON HIM
BECAUSE HE CARES FOR YOU.
1 peter 5:7